BETTER BOUNDARIES:

You Don't Have to Be Broken to Be Better

KARI KWINN

Dear Brooke,

You are already perfect
(but read the book anyway)?

Much love,
Kari

For Hannah, who helped me to know the difference

Prologue

I believe it's important to know that your life can always be better, and it will never be perfect. This book is written from my perspective, and I want to acknowledge that I am one of the luckiest women on Earth. It is written for other such fortunate people who have become paralyzed by their privilege. We have tried to shrink in response to it, rather than growing to embrace and re-allocate it.

If you have excess, you must give it away. That is the nature of things.

Spiderman said the most powerful words I've heard regarding this matter: "With great power comes great responsibility." Do not shy away from it; rise to meet it.

The rest of the book will tell you how.

While it may seem counterintuitive, I believe this book is laid out in such a manner that you will benefit most from reading it from start to finish, even though that is not the way I wrote it.

You'll notice that there are three sorts of writing inside. First, I share a tool or technique that may drastically improve your life by asking you to create a new perspective for yourself. You might enjoy simply reading these sections and getting quite practical.

I include my personal behind-the-scenes narrative of how each tool is useful.

Sometimes context helps lessons find their relevance, and if you are the sort of person who likes to see something in action before saddling up yourself, you may enjoy these sections.

Finally, there are personal interludes. They are my inner voice and represent my feelings and experiences. Even though they are neither tools nor explicit applications, people tell me they enjoyed these parts the most. If you're the sort of person who would prefer to get to know me first before learning the tools, I invite you in.

In homage to Mark Acito, an important writer in my life, I invite those who prefer to jump in willy-nilly to open to any random page and dip your toes in the water. Sometimes God speaks in this way—by responding with precisely what you need to read in the moment. If your belief structure does not include a god, that's just fine. The method works regardless.

Finally, for additional resources and print-outs of exercises mentioned in this book, visit www.createbetterboundaries.com/downloads.

Introduction

Full disclosure: I am writing this book to profit from the ridiculous and marvelous missteps I took trying to figure out who I am in the world and how I relate with other people. The excellent news for you is that I made a variety of intricate mistakes and learned from them. Now that you're reading this, you can hopefully relate to my entanglements and skip some of the drama for yourself.

This book is not for you if...

You are in an abusive relationship. You might determine over the course of reading this that you are in an abusive relationship, in which case you will need to stop reading and get out. Full stop. There is no way to make a relationship work when one person is abusive to the other. I repeat, the only way through an abusive relationship is out.

You are reading this on behalf of someone who could really use it. As you'll read, there are so many ways we can improve our boundaries and so many hilarious and adorable ways our boundaries can be less than ideal. Reading this book to change someone else's boundaries is as adorable as peeing for someone else; somehow, it never works.

You are in active addiction. This means that you keep doing something even though it causes you suffering (see above, regarding the abusive relationship). Addiction could be defined as engaging in an abusive relationship with your substance or behavior or choice. You must stop first; once you are well onto your path of sobriety or recovery, come on back. This will help you rebuild and repair boundaries you may have never known you needed.

You have a mental health condition and are not in regular therapeutic conversation with a licensed professional. Hi. This is a book. It is not a substitute for therapy.

This book is for you if...

You are looking to improve your relationships. They don't have to be broken to be better, but if there are interpersonal dynamics in your life that are less than stellar, this book will help you identify those areas and see how your side of the relationship is malleable. I'll also give you lots of examples and tools to use.

You would like to avoid repeating painful decisions. Have you noticed that you make some of the same self-defeating decisions repeatedly? Maybe you always let your sister borrow your clothes and she never returns them. Maybe you agree to go to a restaurant you dislike with your coworkers in the hopes that someday they'll ask you where you want to go. Maybe you date people who are mean or neglectful. The excellent news about making these types of choices? You don't have to make them anymore.

You have been on a path of self-improvement and would like to add to your toolbox. Whether you've participated in 12-step, other recovery work, therapy, coaching or leadership training, this book will add perspective and tools to your work. It is my belief that life doesn't get easier as you get older but that you do have more tools—and life's hiccups become less distressing when you remember that.

You have nothing better to do. Well, that's a bummer. I'm not sure this book will give you ideas of things to do, but it might help you improve your relationships with family and friends so you get more invitations?

ONE

From Codependency to Boundaries

Codependency is a nasty word. By that, I mean it has negative implications and locks a lot of people into a victim mentality—but It didn't begin that way. It grew up as a term to describe people who were in relationship with active alcoholics. The alcoholic was dependent, the partner/parent/child was codependent, and everybody needed sobriety and recovery. Codependents were under the mistaken idea that if the alcoholic stopped drinking, then all problems would dissolve. The fathers of Alcoholics Anonymous (AA) helped alcoholics realize that alcohol was a symptom of bigger problems, just as Al-Anon has helped codependents realize that their behavior is also a symptom of bigger problems.

Over time, the term codependency has evolved to have a wide range of meanings. Some people who have never had a relationship with alcoholism refer to themselves as codependent. People who have been in active recovery for decades call themselves codependent. It is used to describe anyone who manipulates and controls the behavior of another person in an attempt to help them. The painful lesson of codependency is that manipulation and control never help.

One of my favorite definitions of codependency was coined by Nikki Myers, founder of Y12SR, the Yoga of 12-Step Recovery. Nikki calls codependency "the disease of the lost self." This resonated with me when I was in the thick of a relationship with someone in active addiction, and it helped me see and appreciate the shared nature of my condition. She helped me learn that I was not alone in feeling or behaving the way that I did.

The main reason I dislike the term is the way people use it as an identity rather than a behavior. My personal belief is that people are not born codependent—it isn't an inherent personality type or a dysfunction of anatomy or chemistry. Codependent behaviors are learned and adopted as survival tactics, and because of that, I believe they can be identified and selected against. If you choose to call yourself "a codependent" because the identity helps you to move away from maladaptive behaviors, please go ahead. I prefer not to label people or put them into boxes, but instead to look at their behaviors and support them in living differently. I prefer to have the conversation in relationship to boundaries.

What is a Boundary?

A boundary is an edge, like the membrane of a cell. It is clearly defined and allows certain things in and others out. It's very simple in the world of cell biology, and we can use physical illustrations to apply the concept of boundaries to our lives as well.

Think of homes. Some people live in free-standing houses with a few doors to the outside. They might lock the doors or leave them unlocked, or have an electronic security system. There might be a fence or a gate. Others live in shared buildings. These might have a main entry door, a security system, a door man, and a lock on the door to the individual unit. Castles used to have moats and towers with armed guards. Some homes in tropical parts of the world—even developed parts—are completely open, with free-floating hammocks or mosquito-net-covered beds and interior walls that only support kitchen cabinets or upper floors.

We can apply these same ideas to behaviors; there are things you are willing to do and less willing to do. It is possible to have antisocial behaviors or to over-share, to be closed off like the castle with a moat or very open like the unwalled tropical home. It is up to you.

Healthy Boundaries

I would love to define this for you, but the work of this book is for you to define general boundaries for yourself, and then have a system in place to adapt, refine, and create new boundaries as life presents new circumstances and puzzles. This starts with identifying who you really are, what you really want, which qualities you're willing to work with in others, and which ones you're not.

People with healthy boundaries do not have ongoing experiences of drama or resentment. They resolve conflict quickly, take responsibility for their actions, and don't take things personally.

Less-Healthy Boundaries

We are going to become experts at identifying areas where our boundaries need more work. For example, when you feel resentment, put your foot in your mouth, or get upset because someone didn't do what you wanted them to, this is an indication that you have transgressed your own boundary. Resentment reminds you that you've been ignoring your own needs, wants, or preferences, or that you've been keeping them quiet rather than sharing them with others. You might be doing it to be polite or to make life simpler, but if you're feeling resentment, you're doing it at the expense of your own peace.

Feeling mired in drama and helpless to escape is another good indication of underdeveloped boundaries, even (and especially) if it feels like the drama is silly and futile and you should "just get over it." Jealous of your best friend? Irrationally irritated by your child's music teacher? Picking fights in social media circles? You're diverting your energy away from where it's needed and towards something futile, and you're stuck.

There are a lot more clues, and the excellent news is when we find them, we can change our behavior.

But I Want to Be In Control

I so relate to this. I often think I want to be in control (even my lists have lists), but the unfortunate reality is that we usually can't control circumstances involving other people or entities. While the ways we try to take control may vary, many of them are attempts to soothe ourselves and create a different emotional state of safety, calmness, or relaxation. We can't control our circumstances, but we can control our behavior and our responses to them.

Your Behaviors Are Not Your Identity

One of the best decisions I have made is to separate my behaviors from my identity. This is not to excuse crummy behavior but to look at my behavior objectively and avoid feeling resignation. Resignation in your inner dialogue sounds like, "Oh well, I guess I'm just screwed up and this is proof!" Instead, that voice could sound like, "I am starting to engage in my adorable codependent behaviors—I can stop now!"

Interlude: A Year

One year ago, I walked into an Al-Anon meeting.

In the previous month, I'd been to all sorts of 12-step meetings, looking for my home. The pamphlets didn't describe me. In some, the people gaped at me with hungry eyes: fresh meat.

The last night of the year I ended up at an AA meeting because an angel came and found me. I was there, wandering around the church annex looking for another meeting, but apparently, I was the only one, and the loneliness of being stood up by other anonymous addicts in my tribe was intolerable.

A man popped out of the AA meeting down the hall and asked if that's what I had been looking for. When I said no and he saw my face, he invited me in, and they welcomed me home.

My friend Hannah calls me an "honorary alcoholic"—not because I have a substance abuse issue, but because my disease has the same ancestry. My delicate constitution has prevented me from ever truly overindulging in alcohol, but my spirit has always been insatiably thirsty in the same way.

(Maybe yours has too?)

My codependency had started as a distraction from the

incredible pain of infertility, and it followed me to the Bahamas, to the ashram, where I was supposed to get clear *and* get healed, *or at least insulate myself from inflicting my poisonous thoughts and feelings on the healthy masses.*

I sat there, night after night, in dark meditation, surrounded by 300 strangers and the sweet song of the Caribbean, convinced I had been infected.

(And I had been, just not with a disease for which there is a pill.)

My self-worth eroded by infertility, my resilience depleted, I had become the perfect host.

Infected by addiction.

The years that followed were the worst of my life, because I was simultaneously consumed by how much I despised myself, and by how much I realized my behavior would likely kill me.

Was I hoping to live or die?

(Both.)

All addiction breeds rage, which is fed by shame, which continues to multiply with each uncontrollable grasping for The Thing that will never fill the hole.

It starts with I believe there is a hole in me *and that there will be A Thing that will fill it. But it won't; not because it can't, but because the hole is a lie. It is a ghost—an apparition.*

And it's hungry.

My addiction became him, his behavior, his pathological inability to find or speak "the truth," and I was lost. Consumed by tracking, by living a double life, a deranged fulfillment of my Sherlockian roots, my anthropological leanings, my stubbornness.

The strong female leads of my childhood gone seriously wrong.

He left. I left. There were lines in the sand.

The people of Al-Anon sat with me in the dark moments, hearing the horror stories bleached of unsavory details and nodding. Saying things about hope and courage and focusing inwards. We have been lost too, their eyes said. Some of us lose ourselves on the daily. And yet we believe you can find you again, as we have also found ourselves on this path.

This past year has been about me—*this next year will be about* me. *It started with realizing that there was never a hole, that this was simply the topography of my garden. Then a fence, then weeding and now intentional planting. Fence maintenance. Ongoing weeding. Nurturing* what comes next.

Alice in Wonderland so plainly spoke it, the sentiment of my sisters in Al-Anon. "When you can't look on the bright side, I will sit with you in the dark."

Thank you, my unknown darlings, who heard my desperation and didn't try once to fix it. You simply sat outside and watched me build my own fence, clear my own wreckage, build my new life.

TWO

It Depends

One of the greatest yogic teachings has been transmitted to me via at least a dozen different teachers. The answer to every question is, "It depends." I find this to be true not as an escape from providing an answer, but as a reminder that we have authority and autonomy to make decisions based on everything we know about a particular circumstance.

I teach this with the phrase: "There is more than one right way to do everything." This is a consistent reminder that my approach isn't the "right" or "only" way, and that I might benefit from reflection and consultation.

The essence of codependency is an unhealthy way of engaging with others. To understand codependency, it helps to understand dependency. So, let's look at the ways one can be dependent.

Dependency Is Where We Start

Infants and people who are ill or injured are often dependent on others to meet their basic needs. Human infants cannot articulate their needs—just feeling states—so parents and caregivers anticipate and support their needs. A person who is physically ill or injured might experience similar dependency, needing help to feed themselves or bathe even though they can often express their needs, wants, and desires through language. In both cases, it is critical that someone provide the care needed for these individuals to survive. Ideally, when we transition in and out of states of dependency with those we love, we do so with clearly defined needs and boundaries for starting and stopping.

Codependency can seem like caregiving but is often called caretaking, where a person anticipates another's needs and provides for them without an agreement that care is needed.

Anti-dependence is a quality that can develop in protest to caretaking. In an attempt to assert independence, we refuse support and want to do things ourselves. Running away is an expression of anti-dependence, but often reminds us that we cannot take care of 100 percent of our needs by ourselves. We are pack animals and cultural beings, and most of us live in environments where it is exceptionally difficult for a human to live solo without any aid from others.

We Seek Independence

Independence is a little tricky. We may unconsciously develop unhealthy boundaries as we seek independence. Ideally, healthy adults can operate independently and make decisions for themselves. They know who they are and can easily identify their own wants, needs, and preferences.

Interdependence is where boundaries really shine. An interdependent relationship is made of two or more independent people who collaborate. They feel safe to express their needs, wants, and preferences and can be in and out of the group equally well, each compromising and contributing to each other's betterment in a healthy way. More work gets done in healthy interdependence without drama.

Codependency

Codependency feels dramatic because it is. Rather than reaching common goals, accomplishing work, or creating sense of intimacy, a codependent relationship is fueled by drama. Red flags include masks, lies, control, and manipulation. It often happens when the people involved have an unsteady sense of independence. They share the perception that one person is dependent upon the other when, in fact, this is not true.

Codependency often looks like two people in a lifeboat in the middle of the ocean. They feel completely isolated and fully reliant on one another—

and in the case of addiction, one person is trying to chop holes in the hull and light the whole thing on fire while the other tries to keep it afloat. If you believe one person is your everything and you couldn't make it without them, or if you believe one person is your project and your life would be meaningless without them, it may be codependency.

Codependency can take many forms. For example, maybe the person contributing the money has more power because the other person depends on them for financial support. Feeling or behaving in a dependent way invites the other person to control and manipulate. In a healthier, interdependent relationship, both people are working towards a common goal and each is contributing in an agreed-upon way.

In families or small groups, it's more like there are four or six people in the lifeboat. If everyone in the boat has the same circle of support and nobody looks outside, chance are there are some crummy behaviors or thoughts circulating. Sometimes a family decides to keep a secret, and everyone plays an important role in guarding it. Other times, a peer group engaging in a destructive behavior may not see the gravity of their actions because everyone in the boat is doing it too.

I define codependency as "saving someone from the consequences of their actions." If you are piercing a hole in your lifeboat and I am mending the hole, I am saving you from the consequences of your actions. I did this for years before I remembered that I could swim—and I don't deserve to spend my life fixing someone else's lifeboat.

Boundaries foster a healthy sense of indepen-dence, which allows you to engage with others confidently.

People Are Not Their Behaviors

Our language and culture invite us to identify with our actions, roles, and behaviors. This doesn't always lead to our best health and wellness. As I said, I believe people are not their behaviors; behaviors are habits or coping methods that have served us in some way or were learned from watching others or the media. They are not necessarily conscious choices.

One way I remind myself and others that we are not our behaviors is to use the word "adorable." When I notice myself worrying about my friend who is traveling, if I can see my worry as "adorable," I can separate myself from it and the shame I feel knowing that worry is unproductive. If I sit down to write and notice I'm cleaning off my desktop, shopping for rugs I don't need, or picking a fight on social media, I can recognize my adorable procrastination behavior, pat it on the head, and make a different choice.

I also use this to distinguish the severity of the behavior and whether I might want to address it with a support team. I can address my adorable procrasti-nation tendency with a technology tool, like a timer or a sticky note on my computer that says, "Focus for 20 minutes—you've got this!"

Compare this to secretly drinking a bottle of Chardonnay after everyone else goes to bed. While I am still not my behavior, this would feel less adorable —less like I can pat it on the head and more like something I might want to tell another living human about. When in doubt, tell someone. Especially if you don't want to.

Over the course of the book, you'll see this word and very practical tools to support you in changing your behaviors in a way that best serves you. If you start to uncover secret or less-than-adorable behaviors, I commend you for the excavation and implore you to seek counsel to discuss them sooner rather than later.

A great place to start evaluating your behaviors is to look at them from a 12-step perspective. While many of us quickly identify substances as potentially detrimental, we don't always look at our boundaries with belongings, money, food, sex, time, work, people, and technology. Peruse the list below to see if there are any items on it you identify with that make your stomach turn:

- Hoarding
- Shopping
- Spending
- Eating Sugar
- Regulating food
- Binging
- Watching porn/internet sex
- Masturbating
- Over-using dating apps
- Overscheduling

- Double-booking
- Over-working
- Under-earning
- Helicopter parenting
- Caretaking
- Being hypervigilant
- Scrolling social media
- Obsessing over news

If you are using substances in a way that hasn't been prescribed for you by a person with medical credentials, or if you are using them in secret, please stop reading and go get support. You cannot address any other aspect of your life until you have addressed this one—it's like attending to the creaking doors or running toilet while the house is on fire.

Interlude: Puzzle Pieces

Yoga teaches us that we are supposed to be unique, special, and powerful pieces of a whole, that our part in the universe is infinitesimally small and essential. The universe, as it is, cannot survive without our existence for whatever time we are here to exist. We have a purpose, and that purpose is to figure out our purpose.

Big, right?

I think of it like a jigsaw puzzle. I used to love puzzles when I was a kid, collecting and assembling with my father on late, cold, dark nights with tea and minimal conversation.

If you haven't sat with a puzzle in a while, I'll remind you of the rules.

Each piece is a unique, special part of the whole. The piece is infinitesimally small and essential. The puzzle cannot be complete without it. The point of the puzzle is to put all the pieces in their special place, or work at finding their special place.

Huh.

Same.

If you have ever sat down with a toddler or small child who doesn't know the rules, you can see their adorable attempts at stuffing pieces together. They might sit with extreme frustration, trying to make something fit that doesn't. You—as the observer—can see precisely how the piece doesn't fit. The edges are the wrong shape, or they are missing critical bits. Industrious toddlers will sometimes attempt to modify the pieces (by biting off sections) to force a fit.

We do this in life.

If our whole goal is to figure out how we fit (our purpose), we must start by getting very clear on our edges, or boundaries. This is a new idea if we were raised in a culture that suggests cutting off parts of ourselves or adding on new parts will be a great way of establishing a fit. Like the toddler, we must stop hacking away at our edges and instead know, define, and articulate them.

Experiences we have in life will help us learn about our edges and boundaries. As we bump up against people, situations, and entities, we will notice things that fit and things that don't. We will have feelings.

All of this is part of the process.

We are so lucky to have the insight of the adult watching the toddler. We can watch and see this discovery unfold, experience the adorable missteps, and gently guide ourselves back to the process rather than forcing a fit that damages ourselves or others.

THREE

Higher Council
_____

Have you ever wished that you had a panel of advisors who knew you intimately, who were experts in their fields, and who wanted the best for you?

If you haven't, I encourage you to consider how much better your life could be with a board of experts there to help you navigate and make informed decisions, recognize your adorable patterns, and possibly avoid some of the painful scenarios in which you find yourself.

Read on.

First—a reminder. You absolutely must advocate for yourself. The house always wins. This is what they say about casinos because the casino would not be in business if it were possible for it to lose money. The casino presents all opportunities for you to spend money in such a way that they always earn money. Despite what you may think, I'll suggest that this isn't evil and is instead an excellent teacher.

In your life, you must be the house. You must

create scenarios that have your best interests in mind, because no one else will do this for you. If you are an independent adult, no one else ought to be making decisions on your behalf, guessing what it is that you need or want.

And?

Left to your own devices, with only your perspective, you're likely to make bad decisions or get stuck in a loop. Your tendency might be to trust your inner voice above all, avoid input because of pride or fear, or let chance take the wheel. Your inner wisdom is wonderful, but it can sound quite a lot like your adorable tendencies, so it's often beneficial to check in with someone who isn't you. Or a few someones.

You already have this—all of us have those we consult—but sometimes these people tell us what we want to hear, or sometimes we ask them about areas of life where they know no more than we do. I did this for years.

My friend Bob is remarkable. He is so proficient at so many things that I one day realized I would text him for literally any question. *How long can I leave the dog in the car? How do you bake a chicken? I'm updating my website—can you help me with the SEO? I'm looking to refinance my house—how do I do that?* Legitimately all questions I asked him, and because he is so incredible, he had good, substantive answers for all of them.

But even Bob isn't an expert at everything, and what I was doing was leveraging our friendship too much—I was asking more of him than was probably reasonable without compensating him in some way.

So, I sat down to do what I'm asking you to do: I drew my circle of support.

First, I drew a dot in the middle (me). Then I made a pie chart of the different areas of my life where I could use support: family, work, health, home, fitness, recovery, pet care.

Then, I sat down and wrote names in the various areas based on who might have a level of expertise in any one of these areas.

The chart was…thin.

There was a lot of 1-800-ASK-BOB happening in my life, so I scrolled through my recent text messages to see how I might round out this support team. Then I rearranged people into "closer" and "farther" circles. The closest circle was people I could text at 9 pm who were likely to respond, the middle circle was people who would likely get back to me within 24 hours and the outer circle was professionals.

As you do this, you'll see there are sections that are quite robust and other areas where you have a few vacancies. Maybe a lot of vacancies. Maybe 100 percent open real estate.

This is good news.

The innermost circle might have only three people who cover a broad range of categories because they are peers or siblings. They are the closest go-to people when you hear a noise across the house after dark, or discover that your dishwasher is exploding, or get a DM on your brand-new Instagram account from someone who ghosted you.

"Hey…you just popped into my feed…how ya been?"

The middle circle should be robust. Think of these people as peers with a little bit of expertise in a particular area—mentors. Maybe you really admire your friend Jen's parenting techniques and your friend Larry's garden. Maybe you are in recovery or in a faith group, and some of the folks are peers on the path who would be happy to chat with you about a problem. Fill them in.

The outer circle are professionals. Your physician, veterinarian, landscaper, therapist, and accountant are in this circle. Again, note that people like your veterinarian are not necessarily your friends, but rather people you have established a professional relationship with and selected for consultation when the need arises.

Evaluate

Take a step back and see where you have vacancies. Also note if there is a section you've forgotten or avoided (like, for most people, sex). Maybe you are struggling with a question right now—a career change, end-of-life care for a family member, infertility—and you had not even considered asking for support or help in this area. Create the slice of pie, and let's get to work.

When I teach my course on how to do this, I love to have people share their charts, even if I cannot read the names or the subjects. I often see charts with a cluster really close to the middle and no professionals, or one that is all pros and no informal consultation. I also see some where there is one prominent person blobbing all over the whole chart. It's awesome. Whatever your chart looks like, you can change it. Quickly. I'll show you how.

Dream

When I did this, I had Bob and my crew of hired help —acupuncturist, doctor, dermatologist, dentist, lawyer, accountant. I was clearly very professional, but I never realized that I functioned primarily as an expert for other people without identifying the "right" people to lean on when I had a question. This resulted in me asking the wrong people the wrong questions—asking Bob or not asking anyone.

So, I started to dream. I wrote down my ideal team, and I renamed them my higher council. I included Dharma (from the hit '90s TV show *Dharma & Greg*) as a close confidant, Oprah for business advice, and a famous photographer I could never afford as my photographer.

And I encourage you to do the same. For all vacancies, dream about a fictional character, a celebrity, a notable person who could fill the role. Write the person's name in that spot and indicate that they are a space holder with another color or an asterisk.

Assemble

Now, get on with your life and see who comes in. I'm not a huge fan of "the law of attraction" as it is typically taught—that you just need to think really, really hard, manifest, or make a collage of Oprah magazines and one day, Oprah will walk into your local coffee shop and offer you business advice. But I do believe that it is easier to recognize what we are looking for if we know what it looks like.

I found my Dharma, my Oprah, and my photographer simply by living my life and being open to meeting them. My tendency had been to stay in my house and never leave unless someone paid me, which made it difficult to meet new people. So, I started going out more, saying "yes" to coffee dates, library talks that interested me, and classes I didn't normally attend. I came to yoga early and stayed late to chat with the people nearby, in search of candidates for my higher council.

I found my Dharma (Hannah) at a coffee date I should never have attended. My boss at the time invited me to a coffee date at Deus Ex Machina in Venice Beach. If you're not familiar, Deus Ex Machina is a chain of biker/coffee bars in many chic locations around the world, which would have made for a lovely little outing to begin with. Motorcycles and coffee? What fun to write home about.

But the Latin phrase *deus ex machina* (God from the machine) refers to a plot device that saves the protagonist from a hopeless situation. While I was far from hopeless, the synchronicity was not lost on me. Hannah looks modestly like Jenna Elfman (who played Dharma)—bohemian, leggy, blonde—but her life was so much more like Dharma's than anyone I'd ever met. I couldn't have picked a better fit for my HC.

Oprah came to me in the form of two different people, one of whom actually appeared on the Oprah show. One offers money coaching for people who work in the nebulous world of self-help, and one advises those who need help mustering up a sense of self-worth (which I believe is almost everyone). These women helped me locate an intimacy coach who, along with therapy and 12-step work, helped me unearth the most basic and uncomfortable truths I was hiding.

And the photographer?

I met two.

Seriously.

Use

Your HC will never be perfect. It will never be full; it is a template and a map to use in moments of crisis or evaluation when you are seeking support. Please don't wait for it to be full before you start to use it.

How you use it will depend on so many factors, but assembling it is the first step. Then, next time you're ruminating over a tough choice, feel like you could use some counsel, or are just wanting to practice asking for help rather than hermit-ing, consider reaching out.

"Hey, Tim, I was wondering if you had a few minutes to chat with me about my upcoming trip? I hear you're a pro at international travel, and I'd love some packing tips."

Easy, low-risk, low-investment ask. Try it out.

He might say no, in which case, you find someone else you could ask and repeat. Get tips from a few people, even if you think you're the world's greatest packer. The point is to practice using the council on something that's relatively insignificant.

You're practicing for the moment when you start contemplating divorce, or your child tells you they want to go to college and you don't have experience applying, or you inadvertently win big at the casino and don't know how to manage your windfall.

Another great thing your HC can do for you is listen. When you reach out, you need to know if you're looking for an ear or advice. Are you contacting them because they're great at listening to you process how terrible your boss just was, or because they have tips they might be willing to share? Tell them whether you're asking for an ear or advice.

"Do you have 15 minutes to listen to me vent about my boss? I'm struggling and need to get the words out of my head so I can think. I'm not looking for advice about what to do, just a kind ear. Are you free?"

They may say no, which is why you've built out your council.

How to Find a Therapist

First, determine which area of your life is most problematic. Look at your higher council diagram as it is today and notice if there are any particular vacancies. Relationships? Money? Family? Work? Addiction? Compulsive behavior? Start there. Research therapists in your area using the following methods. Unless you currently have a therapist who is really rounding out your needs, this is a worthwhile exercise.

If nothing rises to the top but you're sort of *meh*, find someone who specializes in trauma and EMDR. If you are one of the eight people on Earth who has no history of trauma, they will let you know and point you in the direction of the unicorn therapist.

Establish the Qualities You Value in a Therapist

Aside from finding someone with the right professional credentials, sharing the same basic value system as your therapist is important. Oh, you don't already have a list of your own core values? Google "list of values" and choose some! Find five to 10 that are your non-negotiable values. Then spend five minutes with each one, free-writing what that value means to you. Mine include integrity and humility. It is vital that my therapist possess these qualities.

Integrity to me is owning your mistakes, asking for help, being willing to be wrong and being willing to go against the grain. It means standing up for what you believe and allowing other people to believe differently. It means your behavior does not keep you up at night.

Humility to me is constant learning, an interest in self-improvement, and owning that you are a small, essential piece of something much, much larger. It means you can say "Please," "I'm sorry," "Thank you," and "Tell me more about that."

Establish the Intolerable Qualities of a Therapist

It is critical that you define and redefine this list. Does the physical affect of the person matter to you? For instance, if you're trying to work through your relationship with your father, you might want someone who is older than you and reminds you of him or you might want someone who looks nothing like him. It's completely okay to have this on your list for a relevant reason. Interrupting is a big one for me—I want someone who lets me finish my thoughts and then has something to offer, not someone who jumps in (I interrupt often, by the way; I'm aware of it, and I'm working on it). If you live in a small town or have an intimate community, you might like to eliminate people who are part of that community so you don't rely on someone you see at the Bingo hall every Friday.

Use the Force

The internet is very good for this, as are your personal relations. If you happen to have a peer or mentor in this area of your life, you might let them know that you're in search of a therapist and ask if they know anyone. If you have a friend who is a therapist, you can ask them to refer you to other therapists who might be a good fit. You don't want to see your friend as a therapist; you could invite them into a non-clinical role on your HC, but it's best to find a new and unassociated person. If it is not important to see your therapist in person, you can expand your geographical area. You can refer to your insurance coverage to see who is in your network or most affordable.

Caveats

One big mistake people make with the HC exercise is to allow pirates into their council. The council is appointed by you, not by the people within it. Maybe your Aunt Z is a champion at unsolicited advice. She knows just what to do to fix your hair, find you a mate, get you a high-paying job, and fix your roof.

But if you didn't put her on your HC, she doesn't belong there, and you don't have to take her advice.

These people often start with the phrase, "You know what you should do…"

You can listen, or you can stop them. But you don't have to let the advice in. You can let it fly over your head like the adult voices in Charlie Brown, off into the ether, or you can say, "Aunt Z—I appreciate you so much. I'm not asking for your advice."

Pirates can be contained in appropriate sections of the HC. Maybe Aunt Z is the best gardener, and she's lonely so she reaches out to give you advice on everything. It isn't malicious, even if it feels like all she does is pick at you. She's lonely. She has no HC of her own. Help her help you by asking her about gardening. Encourage her to build out her own HC and suggest she share her awesome gardening advice with people who really need it.

Reciprocity

One big mistake people make with the HC is imagining that they must reciprocate with their people. While some form of reciprocity is useful, I think many people delay or avoid asking for help because they don't know what it will cost them. I prefer to think of paying into a system and receiving from a system rather than focusing on the one-to-one reciprocity.

Also, this is why money exists.

If you feel like you are asking for a favor, be clear about what you are asking for and leave space for the person to say no. If you are asking someone about their profession, expect to compensate them with money.

Your doctor is on your higher council, but you're likely not on theirs, right? And you don't feel strange about that arrangement because you pay your doctor. If you have a friend who is a lawyer, you don't contact that person as a member of your HC to ask for legal advice unless you are prepared to pay for it. Lawyers and doctors get this all the time, and it isn't equitable. What is reasonable is to ask for a referral.

"Hey Rob, you're a lawyer. I just got this letter and am wondering if you can refer me to a reasonable lawyer who manages this sort of thing. Can you connect me?"

Or, "Hey Rob, you're a lawyer. I just got this letter and would love to come see you about it. Can you please let me know the best way to schedule so I see you and not one of your partners?"

Money is how we make these sorts of relationships equitable. They set their price, and we find the right fit. It's about being confident about who you are and clear about what you're asking for.

If someone asks you to be on their HC, you always get to say yes or no. And in order to operate skillfully, you'll want to be sure your HC is in tip-top shape first. We can only give from our excess, so be sure you're well supported before you start offering support.

Also remember that someone can be on your HC in one area, even if another area of their life is a mess. Your acupuncturist might have tremendous insight about your health and well-being, giving you excellent recommendations about rest and diet, *and* she might have a very difficult time keeping her plants alive. She is of great service in one way and not in another. Some examples like this are very clear, but it is worth reviewing areas of your life to see where you're asking one person to advise you in an area in which they are really a novice.

Repeat

Your HC will evolve over time. If you have children, their needs are likely to change as they mature. If you have parents, their needs are likely to change as they mature. If you hit hiccups in life, change careers, or want to learn a new skill, your HC will need to adapt to best support you in that moment. It isn't a static system; instead, it is a garden that requires a little attention to bear fruit.

Mentoring

It can feel so nice to be asked for help that we will often offer support out of flattery instead of admitting that our skill set is not as robust as the requesting party believes it to be. Even so, offering our skills to others when they could actually be of use can be incredibly rewarding. Once you feel your ship is sailing well, take inventory of each area of your life. Where can you offer mentoring or support? You will know you can be a mentor to others when your HC is pretty steady and populated by a diverse group of actual humans. Conversely, where are you unable to lend an ear or some time? If you're clear on your own areas, you can skillfully help others yourself or at least help them find the right support.

While "no" is a valid, reasonable, and perfectly acceptable answer to a request for help, you might consider saying "no" but offering a suggestion. If you are a retired midwife, people might want to know how to best support their friend who is expecting. Maybe you have some advice, but you're tired of giving it out. Maybe your information is outdated. It's reasonable to offer these explanations and then suggest a book, resource, or couple of questions they might ask another person to find their answers.

Secrets

Is there something in your life you can't tell anyone?

That's totally valid. It's valid that there are things you do not want to tell anyone, and that is a sure-fire way to ensure things continue the way that they are, which might be fine. But also? It's not fine.

Secrets are a lie. They are an example of a very bad boundary imparted by someone who was unskillful (thoughtless or reactive) or even abusive. Secrets are cancerous to your emotional and spiritual bodies, and as they say, secrets do not make friends.

Think of the one thing that you really don't want anyone to know. If nothing comes to mind, think about the extra weird things you might do to cover your tracks after shopping. The way you might brag about how little sleep you need, or how little time you spend on social media, or the food you eat in your car. Anything you cannot put in the garbage at home because a roommate or family member might uncover it. In which area of your life do you leave no trace?

Don't have secrets?

If there is a part of your life where you believe

you are your best and only advisor, this is another way of saying it is a secret. Certainly, you have information about yourself that no one else has, but attempting to manage a situation like compulsive spending, eating, or masturbation on your lonesome is not going to work. Even less skillful than this is believing you are the only person who can provide this support for another person (this is the other half of the secret). Whether there is no one you want to tell or you are the only person someone *else* can tell, what you are dealing with is ticking loudly.

Don't believe me?

Say you notice that your partner has persistent nosebleeds and they are quite embarrassed about them. They ask you not to tell anyone because it's a tender subject and they have their pride to defend. It doesn't seem like a big deal to you, so you keep it to yourself and notice the way your partner starts to manage around this inconvenience. They are less social and more withdrawn. They are dismissive of you when you inquire about them. It perks your hypervigilance and you start to notice more, and research more, and ruminate more. Is it:

> *A: Cocaine?*
> *B: A brain tumor?*
> *C: A nose-picking compulsion?*

The answer is D: not your job to diagnose or treat, but kudos for your creative thinking!

But also: not your job to keep the secret. It doesn't

mean you immediately call your sister or passive aggressively post on social media, but maybe you agree to keep the nosebleeds private between you, your partner, and their chosen licensed healthcare professional. If your partner refuses to seek treatment, you get to leverage your higher council and consult your therapist, sponsor, and/or clergy person. If your hypervigilance is in overdrive, you shouldn't take rash action on your own. By leveraging your HC, you gain useful perspective.

Invite Joy

The law of attraction, vision boarding, and *The Secret* are all lovely ideas, but they aren't always skillfully applied because it is possible to sit down and create a vision board or Pinterest of craving, rather than one motivated by joy. In doing so, one will be caught in an unending loop of looking for just the right silverware, car, and picture-perfect vacation, all of which will feel quite hollow once located or achieved.

Instead, you want a board made of sunsets.

(Not literally).

I made a joy room. At the point in my life when I realized I had completely lost track of what I enjoyed, I needed to make a life raft of things I loved and adored. I cleared everything out of the study and shopped around the house, looking for things that brought me joy I could use to refill the room. Things that made me feel something when I held them, or looked at them, or thought about their story.

I did not go binge shopping at Pottery Barn. I selected from what I already had. Then, I set a policy that only things that brought me joy could enter the Joy Room. If I was on a phone call that got heated, I left the room.

Only. Joy.

It does not have to be a room in your home, nor do I believe you need to fold your shirts and socks like tidying expert Marie Kondo suggests. But she is on point by directing you towards owning less and appreciating more. No more buying a sweater on the clearance rack because it is "good enough," and no more craving the hippest gear for the season unless it also brings you a sense of joy.

If you can fill your home with joy, do so. You don't have to do this by adding more joy; you can do it by getting rid of the lackluster, the tired, the functional but inessential. I do actually love my can opener—it is turquoise. And I love the $3 blanket I bought in India and like to sleep with it next to my face. I love the smell of the camping blanket that cost $10, and the vial of sand from the Ganges makes my heart smile, because it reminds me of a moment.

I principally purchase clothing and housewares from consignment stores now. I don't have to worry about what is on sale or buying eight of something to get a deal. I buy it because it feels nice, or fits well, or meets a need—like getting fancy for a business meeting in London.

I have different relationships with the ex-men in my life. With some, I can look at something they have given me and remember the moment or the person with fondness and without craving. With others, I must get rid of the thing—shred, burn, gift, demolish. But it doesn't get to live in my house, even if it is useful or lovely because seeing it reminds me of a time in my life that I'm not interested in visiting. This is also true with "family heirlooms" that I once felt obligated to hold onto. Infertility has been a gift, telling me that I'm responsible for handing off these items intentionally, not holding onto them for some fabled children I'll never have. Each item can have its own legacy, and I'm not bonded to it 'til death.

Just until I'm ready.

This might well be true in your life, too.

If everything you live with evokes a feeling state, you are doing it right. If not, try using this lens, endeavoring to thank the thing and get it to a home where it does. This is one of the reasons I love consignment shopping and selling—it allows each item to go back to the great cosmic recycler, and it allows me to get what I need when I need it. In my estimation, it is the true embodiment of the temporary nature of life and existence, and what a lovely reminder.

Interlude: Joy

Joy disappeared first, but she went quietly, and so it was a year or more before I realized she'd gone off trail, and I resigned myself to the fact that she was lost forever.

(I felt lost forever.)

I did not find joy or salvation in a man.

(Spoiler.)

But I couldn't have found him without her. And this is the room I devoted to her safe return. This room was my yellow ribbon of faith, my "missing" poster and the bowl of milk I left out during the longest winter nights when God would wake me early and I would pray or try to.

She would visit in my delirium, leaving whisker-prints in milk and fairy dust.

This room became my altar and my haven, a living dream-catcher who had a stronger backbone than I had at the time.

She is a permanent fixture in my life.

A reminder that I'm responsible for my own experience, and that if I seek joy, I'd better make her feel welcome.

There is a difference between craving and joy, and I'm going to make it so simple for you:

Joy is being fully engulfed in a moment—the experience of a sunset. The experience is whole and complete, and you do not immediately get on a plane looking for another one.

Craving feels like a chase, a loop, or a pattern that involves a high and some misery.

You have experienced joy and bliss on many occasions in your life. Maybe the first time you saw the ocean, or held a puppy, or tasted something really tremendous like a mango. Can you think of 100 of these?

I sure hope so because they are the greenest of the green, and like the shimmer of northern lights, they are here to guide you home.

FOUR

Compromise

Most people think they're pretty skilled at compromise yet struggle in real life. Don't believe me? Tell me what usually happens when you need to decide what to do for dinner.

Which do you do?

> *A: Just decide*
> *B: Resign to letting someone else decide*
> *C: Suggest three things and let someone else pick their favorite*
> *D: Guess what you think the other person wants and suggest that*
> *E: Alternate (odd days/even days, flip a coin)*

None of these is a compromise.

It's true that they might work, and it might be true that it's easy to get dinner using one of these strategies, but it isn't developing a skill or tool because you cannot apply the same strategy to sex or a relative's end-of-life care. If you pick A, B, or D, it's likely that someone is experiencing resentment. And while you can decide to let resentment go, most people don't. Most people let resentment build until it is overwhelming, and then they explode.

I call this "living at the edge of tolerable," and if you can relate, this tool will change your zip code.

To truly use compromise as tool, each party involved in making a decision must know and articulate what they want; it's a simple but critical distinction in building this skill. Choosing what to do for dinner is a great place to examine this because it's low risk— all solutions are reasonably okay. Yet with the overabundance the world offers to many of us, we can still become so wound up in entitlement over choosing what to eat that the process ends in tears and misdirected rage.

If you are the sort of person who learned at a young age to suggest three places you want to eat and let your dining partner select, you're on the path to resentment. This strategy is wonderfully effective for decisions that have no impact on your future and usually breeds less resentment, but if you alternate, you may get into a habit of maliciously choosing the thing you know the other person doesn't want or trying to please the other person by guessing what they want.

Let's look at why these types of decision-making fall apart.

I Just Decide

If you are the only person in the decision-making process who can assert your opinion because the other people are toddlers, you get a pass. Making decisions on behalf of toddlers is your responsibility, and kudos for not letting them vote as they are likely to say "socks" or "Disneyland," and the endeavor will end in tears. If, however, you are dealing with adults, teens, and younger children (with discretion) and are always making the decision, you're likely fostering some adorable behaviors and resentments in your compatriots.

Other cognitively functioning adults get to know and articulate what they want just like you do, and you get to ask them. For teens and younger children, you might try a hybrid option: if they could have anything at all for dinner, what would it be or where would they go? Introduce the concept as a game that you all get to play together. In this game, one person suggesting pizza from Domino's down the street and the other suggesting sushi from 18th-century Japan are both equally valid, because both provide equal opportunity to get to the root of the issue. Which leads to the second question.

Why do you want to go there for dinner? "Because I want to use chopsticks." Now you're getting somewhere. In question two, learning that your partner wants to eat with chopsticks but cares less about the cuisine means you have cultivated intimacy. You now know something that is important to them, *and* you know that you don't have to take them to feudal Japan to fulfill their desires. You can make something at home and eat it with chopsticks—and it may not even have to be sushi or Japanese food. It may even be something you wanted to eat the whole time!

Talking through a compromise will get you light years ahead of "you pick three," "I pick one," or the dictatorial "all ways are my ways"—but real compromise when a sense of intimacy is clearly established first.

Anything You Want Is Fine

This is simply not a true statement. The truer statement might be "I'm tired of making decisions. I cannot make one more and I trust you to pick food I will like," or "Nothing is calling to me right now—do you have a strong preference?"

If I just let you decide, I run the risk of decision-muscle atrophy and forgetting what I even want anymore. This is something I often hear from people whose partners have passed and are now confronted with making all the decisions for the first time in so many years. I faced it at the end of a relationship where though I had not consciously abdicated my decision-making abilities, I had also not identified or articulated my decisions clearly (spoiler: that relationship was not good).

You Pick Three, and I'll Select My Favorite

A great, quick option for dinner—nothing wrong with this method when the choices are all reasonable and relatively insignificant. However, you cannot apply this to sexual preferences, which is an area where compromise is critical. You also cannot apply it to medical decisions, or where to live, or whether or not to get a pet. It also doesn't foster intimacy unless you ask me how I came to choose these three seemingly unrelated restaurants, or I ask you why you always choose the way you do.

Guess What You Think the Other Person Wants and Suggest That

I hope this one feels silly, but I appreciate that it might feel uncomfortably close to home. If you have ever found yourself in the position of managing someone else's emotions, you might employ this strategy to avoid outbursts or disappointment.

(It won't work.)

First, you're not a mind reader. You don't know what they want, even if you think you do. Maybe this is the one day that your friend wants tacos. Maybe they heard about a new place opening or just have a hankering to try something new. If you don't practice asking yourself and asking them, you miss out on these tiny opportunities to ask "why."

The way to start navigating compromise is to get clear on what you want and what you don't. You're likely stronger at doing one than the other, but actually engaging in dialogue will help you see the facts rather than your perception.

We Just Alternate

If you have established common tastes with your dining partner, you might enjoy alternating. You might even decide for the sake of simplicity that alternating is the appropriate solution for you, because you prefer not having a lengthy conversation about dinner every night. Even so, while enjoying a dinner you both agree on enthusiastically, you might consider discussing areas in which you don't have common preferences as an opportunity to practice. My ex-husband and I never fought about anything—truly. I raised my voice twice—once when he was deployed and I was afraid, and again during the divorce process. Otherwise, we just agreed and avoided.

Adorable, right?

Make Three Lists: Red, Green, Yellow

The red list is the "under no circumstances" list. Maybe it is a cuisine you despise, a restaurant owned by your ex, or a place that still serves everything in Styrofoam. Ideally, this list is brief but clear. As you create your list, you may see patterns forming.

The green list is the "enthusiastic yes" list. Maybe it's a cuisine you love, a great value for dollar, or an ambiance that makes you feel at home. This list can be *huge*. There are zero limits to the green list. In fact, to be best prepared to compromise, grow your green list as much as you can.

Yellow is everything between. Fine. Acceptable. Maybe not your first choice, but you have no strong feelings one way or the other. You might be able to identify a few places or qualities that fit here, but you don't need to spend a lot of effort building or whittling this list down.

As an example, my red list for restaurants:

- All-you-can-eat buffets (they are a terrible deal for me financially, and if it is all-you-can-eat, it's usually a very low-quality food.)
- Chick-fil-A (even if Barack Obama invited me to lunch, I would not go there.)
- Chili's (I got food poisoning once, and even though I cannot be sure that's where I got sick, I have too much familiarity with the flavor of the food going the other way.)
- Sticky bars (If it is dark, smokey, and I stick to the floor, I am out.)

My yellow list for restaurants:

- Most fast food (I can usually find something I would eat, but it would not be my choice.)
- Most chain restaurants (Again, it's usually

fine, just not the sort of establishment I adore.)

- Most bars (I don't drink alcohol, so it has to be a special reason to venture to a bar. If a friend is in town, there's a company event, or there's some other reason for me to go, I can do it.)

My green list for restaurants:

- A one-off coffee shop that makes their own food (especially if they serve in real mugs and have a fireplace)
- Local places that have excellent salads, homemade salad dressing, roasted veggies and organic meat, dairy, and eggs
- Quiet bars that serve mocktails, kombucha, or tea
- Any place that serves cupcakes

I encourage you to make these lists for restaurants where you live, and then make similar lists for movies you'd like to see, places you'd like to vacation, travel preferences (hotel, camping, luxury) and a few other areas where you likely need to compromise. Many people can make robust food lists but struggle with these other areas, or have the same tendencies across the types of lists (too many reds or no greens).

Many people find that they live on the orange line —the edge of tolerable between their "no" list and their "maybe" list—which isn't a great place to live.

The good news is if you find your lists aren't fully formed, you now know why you might be feeling despair or resentment. In certain areas of your life, you may realize that your red list has vanished—that you've lowered your standards to the point that you no longer have a list in that area, or your list is pretty puny.

For example, when I started dating (for the first time, at age 36), I thought I had a great red list: no active addiction, no serial killers, no Geminis, no one with bad teeth.

Ok, yes, this list reflected my standards at the time. But they were not good standards. An equivalent list might be a restaurant list that excludes only food that poisons you or goes against your religious beliefs. Those may be your standards, but they aren't your true preferences—they are imposed either by your body's needs or your faith's paradigm. You will need to include a few more personalized items.

A student in one of my courses had this very problem, as she had served in the Army in combat zones and had trained herself to eat a wide range of foods she would not have previously considered. If you grew up in a food insecure environment, lived through the harrowing experience of combat, or struggled with an eating disorder, you might hear echoes of this in your red list. If you're not sure, take the red list to your therapist or trusted friend and chat about any patterns they might find obvious that you don't see.

Another common occurrence is "Seinfeld

Syndrome," an exhaustive list of red with little wiggle room for yellow or green. Seinfeld's dating problem was the opposite of mine: he excluded everyone for reasons that might have been more yellow than red—his "orange" zone was expanding in the other direction, making him tolerate almost nothing. Like big hands. A woman who smelled like soup. People who communicated too much or too little. If you have struggled with mystery illnesses, digestive concerns, or eating disorders, you may have amassed an extensive list that's worth re-examining.

You don't need to spend much time on a yellow list. As you practice choosing where to eat with other people, some of their selections might be just okay. Some might find their way onto the red or green list, but many will just fade into the middle.

And the green list can excite you. Once you have established the red list, focus on building the green. See the world as full of possibilities for experiences you can become enthusiastic about rather than a place you need to brace for or tolerate. Practice this everywhere—in the grocery store, in the bookstore, with travel guides. You're not making a list of things you must see and places you must visit, but you are always prepared to answer the question "Where would you like to go?" Whether it's dinner or an all-expenses-paid trip, you'll be ready.

Bookends

The next step in getting what you want is articulating it. It's a private hell to sit with an unfulfilled desire, so you have to move beyond simply *identifying* what would add to your life to *asking* for what you want or making it happen.

We have many reasons for not allowing this, and we've addressed the first big one. The other common reasons:

- People will find my desires stupid, petty, or otherwise unappealing.
- People will think I'm bossy.
- I won't get my way, and it will hurt.
- I hate saying "no."
- I will have to do something I don't want to do.

Let's take these one at a time.

People Will Find Your Desires Stupid, Petty, and Otherwise Unappealing

This is true, and you are just as likely to find their desires stupid, petty, or unappealing. But other people's desires may present you with options you never would have considered for yourself. How can you know you want sushi for dinner if you don't even know sushi exists? On the other hand, imagine that something *you* like, want or desire, like Zelda's Juice

Bar, has just as much potential to inspire someone else to try something they've never experienced...rather than all of you ending up at Tony's Regular Bar again.

And?

If people say unkind things, it is simply an unskillful way to say you aren't a match. This can be painful, but it is also helpful in each of you finding the right match.

People Will Think You're Bossy

Sure. And you might become bossy if you're not careful to remember that compromise means each person needs to both know and articulate what they want, which requires you to ask the other person to articulate what they want. Is that bossy? Maybe. If they want to simply go along with your choice, it might feel bossy for you to prod them into sharing their interests.

You Won't Always Get Your Way, and It Might Hurt

When you are in a group, you are less likely to get your way. It's a numbers game, and if you are honest rather than manipulative, it's possible you won't have as much sway.

But you will have integrity, and having voiced what you do want, you will have given the rest of the group a little more information about yourself.

Imagine your work group likes to go to happy hour every Tuesday and they always go to the same place: Tony's. Maybe it isn't convenient for you or doesn't have food you enjoy, or you'd simply like the opportunity to introduce your work pals to another place you think they would really like. If you never suggest an alternative, they will never consider it. They still might insist on Tony's for their own reasons. Either way, you get to ask them what they like about Tony's, and they get to know you a little better.

I Hate Saying "No"

Toddlers love saying no. After that, we usually want to create some kind of compromise. Sometimes we are punished for saying no, either directly or indirectly, by being isolated or ignored. Abandonment seems extreme for most cases of saying no, but it's a legitimate fear—after all, many of us have lost friendships, missed opportunities, or experienced FOMO (fear of missing out).

It's so hard for people to say no that they often borrow other people's boundaries to do so. Instead of saying "no" or "I don't want to," they say, "I would, but my daughter has soccer," or, "My boss has me working on something urgent," or, "My fiancé has a big day at work and I think he might need my attention afterwards." These things might be true, but they are often things you would set aside for something you really wanted to do. And often, they are not entirely true.

You might have a work obligation, but you plan to zone out in front of the TV for three hours and then cram the obligation in just before midnight. Your daughter has soccer, but you're not planning to stick around for practice, and your fiancé does not need your undivided attention for many hours if you should be participating in your own life instead.

Saying no can be hard, which is why I suggest doing it differently.

Finding the Yes

Say your sister really wants to try a new coffee shop and she invites you along. You love your sister, but you don't want to go. I'm not suggesting you just say no because you don't want to go, but that you explore where the "yes" would be.

In this case, let's say you've just given up coffee for the 12th time this year, and you're trying very hard to stick to it. Going to a coffee shop where you will be tempted by the aroma and the familiar comforts feels really...uncomfortable. Equally uncomfortable? Admitting to your sister that you're trying to give up coffee again, because you know she'll just make fun of you and chide you into drinking it again.

First—it's completely okay to just say no. You do not have to justify your no to me or anyone else. It's a complete response. If saying no feels impossible to you and you tend to justify, I suggest sharing the "yes" instead. Let's triage your sister's invitation out for coffee by breaking down each aspect of the situation.

Green—spending time with your sister and drinking hot beverages! Red—coffee, coffee shops, justifying your desires. Instead of starting with the "no" ("I gave up coffee and I don't want you to make fun of me"), start with "I'd love to see you and have a hot beverage," and then add the red, "*and* I gave up coffee. I'd love your support."

This gives your sister the information that it isn't about her but about the location and some possible baggage. It takes courage. And it states clearly what you desire. From there, she can say yes or no, or maybe ask you why you think she would make fun of you. Or maybe she will be rude and tell you you're a sorry hunk of junk for trying to make different choices related to coffee, in which case you can end the conversation, as it has crossed into the red zone.

Simple, not always easy.

Maybe you don't want to spend time with your sister because she's in a toxic work environment and all she ever wants to do is drone on about how miserable she is. It might be harder to say this, but no less true. Is there green? Is there a "yes" you can share? "I'd love to go get coffee with you, *and* I would love to talk about how summer camp has changed since we were kids."

Maybe your sister is evil and only wants to have coffee with you because she doesn't want to pay for coffee herself. She's going to ask you for money, tell you she's been caffeinating your children, and inform you that she's found a new pyramid scheme that she has taken the liberty of signing you up to sell gift wrap for in July.

That's a red with red flags: no.

But she's my sister. I know. Maybe you share genetics or common history, but that does not obligate you to accommodate her bad behavior. These kinds of decisions are often more difficult than saying "no" to being shanghaied into selling gift wrap—such as refusing to give money to your sibling who is in active addiction. In those cases, I strongly suggest you review the chapter on the higher council, how to select a therapist, and start there. While it feels more complicated, the answer is still no.

Why Not Cost vs. Benefit or Pro/Con?

This is one of my favorite questions when people are making a decision. Why not make a list of pros and cons and simply weigh them against one another?

This can often work well in business or when you are making a decision between things that do not really matter (which washing machine should you buy, for example). In those cases, pro and con your heart out if you feel it is a better system than red/yellow/green, because all washers will wash clothes, you will likely tolerate any brand or style, and you won't even miss features that you don't know exist. Few people will discover a deal-breaking aspect of a washing machine.

In working with companies and organizations, you

are more likely to come across deal breakers. Consider dating.

Pros: wealthy, attractive, fit, intelligent, great professional reputation.

Cons: bad haircut, rude to waitstaff, verbally abusive on the phone.

You can likely make peace with bad hair, and you might imagine the rudeness is due to a bad day. The third one? Cyanide.

You cannot go on a second date with someone who is verbally abusive to another human because they are showing you that they will be verbally abusive with you. It does not matter how attractive, rich, or esteemed they are. If they are berating their veterinarian, that is toxic.

The same is true with an entity, like a job.

Pros: gorgeous office environment, chipper coworkers, tremendous benefits, dream salary.

Cons: inconvenient commute, frequent last-minute travel, requires you to falsify documents as part of your "other assigned duties."

Hi.

If you simply tally the pros and cons, you might not appropriately weigh how falsifying documents (if that goes against your personal ethics) will damage you legally, medically, or psychologically. But really, some cons invalidate all pros.

This is the red list.

This is a boundary.

When we cross into the red list, the cost may be so much greater than a minor cost or inconvenience. It can cost our integrity, and integrity is what lets us sleep at night. When we can't sleep, that's our body sending us a very loud message that whatever is happening is not okay— and without sleep, our quality of life deteriorates quickly. The things that keep me up at night are varied, and there may be a dozen reasons you struggle to sleep through the night —but do not let dabbling in the red list be one of them.

I Will Have to Do Something I Do Not Want to Do

People who tend towards resignation may simply accommodate requests without considering their own needs. For those people, someone else's desires might feel like a personal obligation to do what the other person wants.

Just a reminder: they aren't. The deal is you must know and articulate your desires and the other party must know and articulate theirs.

Hearing what other people want is part of the magic because it stops you from guessing and can remind you to express your needs, which reminds you to identify them.

Occasionally, you will agree to do something that you wouldn't have chosen to do. This is the yellow list. Yellow is a place of neutrality rather than enthusiasm. You'd love to go to the buffet (your green list, though not mine). You're fine with the deli (your yellow list). You're not going to the bar (your red list). The deli is fine because you don't feel resentment about it. You can agree to go there if you also mention that you are interested in the buffet.

Yellow Is Not the Only Way to Compromise; It Is a Tool

The goal is to know and articulate what you want, not to agree to a place that no one really wants to go because it is on everyone's yellow list. Some families have a rule that everyone should be the same amount of miserable, and that is really unskillful and punitive. The point is not to punish anyone. The point is to be discriminate and articulate to avoid everyone's red zones.

If you are having dinner with one other person, you are hopefully going somewhere that is on one person's green list. The larger the group migrating towards compromise, the more likely you'll land in a place that is mostly green and moderately yellow.

When it comes to a decision where there are very few possible negative consequences, like dinner or buying a washing machine, deciding to go with the yellow list is truly just fine.

The Get Out of Jail Free Card

Nothing in life is black or white, and the tool of the red/yellow/green has some grey in it as well. Once you are well-established in what your areas are, and once you have learned how to say "no" with compassion, you can start to bend the rules.

You cannot do this if your boundaries are soft. This is a multi-step process, and this truly is an advanced move—crossing the red line for specific purposes and times, and under very special circumstances.

I call this the "get out of jail free" card.

You can decide if there would ever be a circumstance where you might cross into the red list and agree to something you have created a clear boundary against. For example, you have decided that you will never dog sit for your neighbor ever again. She took advantage of your availability, never paid you and her dog is grouchy. You decided that even if she paid you $500 a day in advance (looking for the green), you would not. But upon seeing paramedics arrive at her house and cart her husband away, you volunteer to watch the dog until a more appropriate sitter can arrive and relieve you.

Or your tweenager is often late for school and asks you for excuse notes so he does not have to sit in detention. You have a strong boundary that you do not write excuse notes for no reason—you have clearly defined the policy for excuse notes (illness requiring a doctor, fever, and other symptoms). And? You have told your tweenager that one time per semester, you will write an excuse note simply because it is requested. He gets one get out of jail free card. When he approaches you, you ask, "Is this the one time you want to use the note this semester?"

It's quite effective.

There are restaurants I would not ordinarily set

foot in, and yet if specific people were to invite me, I would both be terrifically confused at their food preferences and likely go.

Getting out of jail is really just a clarifying use of "starting with the green," as in once a semester or in the event of a truly life-threatening emergency, as above. It is usually established in advance, not in response to a request. It can be guided by ethics and your moral compass rather than your willingness to toss ethics to the side. You might believe that in emergency circumstances, it is appropriate to shift your rules to best support the health and safety of those surrounding you.

The Purple Line

"Everyone has a price," they say.

I don't.

Out beyond the world of the red zone is the purple zone. For many of us, it parallels the morals and ethics of a faith tradition, or the laws of the land we occupy. I don't date serial killers. I don't falsify my taxes. I don't burn my neighbor's house down because she's blocking my view of the mountains.

The purple makes for excellent works of fiction— we love the vicarious experience of people who find themselves in impossible situations, like war dramas or movies like *Indecent Proposal*. We love koans describing time-limited, paradoxical situations—do you push one person onto the train tracks to save the rest of the people on a train?

Occasionally, we find ourselves in these circumstances. Maybe not the train (hopefully not the train), but a place where we are in a financial pickle and believe the only way out is to commit a crime—like tax fraud, robbery, or prostitution. Crisis situations where we walk the line between red and purple are so much more common than we'd like to admit, and they are an invitation to consider our boundaries. That line is often something we are tempted to cross without telling anyone else.

It is the realm of secrets.

The temptation to cross the purple line will be there, either to feed your ego or resolve a dire circumstance. If you get there, pick up the phone and tell someone. We'll get further into this in the next section, but for now, if you are considering a step away from your morals, phone a friend.

Circles

The red/yellow/green method of compromise is possible in more areas of your life than simply where to go for dinner, which washing machine to buy, which treatment plan is best for your beloved, or how to proceed within budget restrictions.

You can apply this method to behaviors.

This is a concept borrowed from the "circles of behavior" tool used in certain recovery circles wherein problematic behaviors can vary widely. These are often called "process" addictions because the problem is a "process" following an everyday, essential behavior rather than a specific substance. Alcohol, heroin, and nicotine are substances, and it's obvious if you have crossed the line with them.

With food, sex, and money, one person's reasonable behaviors are another person's triggers. For that reason, each person is invited to draft their own "circles of behavior" and categorize their own adorable patterns of behavior into:

- Outer circle = normal, non-triggering, everyday activities
- Middle circle = on the way to a problem
- Inner circle = in the problem

For example, for one person, stopping by the bakery on the way to work to pick up a dozen donuts for a meeting is outer circle behavior—fine, not triggering, nothing to write home about. For another person who has a difficult relationship with donuts, it might be a different story. They might know that if they stop by the donut store, they are likely to pick up something for themselves and they might have shame about it. Offering to run this errand might be considered middle circle behavior, because they know they're on the path to eating a dozen donuts before returning to work.

You do not need to be in recovery from any addiction to use this tool to evaluate your own behavior. You can look at behaviors you don't want to engage in (procrastination, gossiping, avoiding eye contact with your neighbors) and trace your steps back to see what you do just before them. Let those behaviors occupy the middle circle and evaluate and refine until you have a clear warning system to help you avoid them.

You may not notice the moment you're procrastinating. In fact, procrastination by definition is wasting time without noticing...so it is a pesky gremlin. But you might notice *afterwards*. And this is my suggestion: to start observing these behaviors by reflecting on your day every evening. Look back at where the time went and start to collect data on your middle circle behaviors. If you landed in front of the TV, the internet, or the spice cabinet (which you were anxiously cleaning), backtrack to the moments that led to it.

There was a time in my life when my partner was deployed to a combat zone. I worked an 8 am to 5 pm job, then went to the gym, then sat in front of the TV and watched endless hours of mediocre television. Sounds typical, right? Nothing really wrong with it at all. Certainly not an addiction! Except it wasn't what I wanted to be doing with my life. I wanted to read books, write books, and enjoy my youth. But every night, I would find myself in front of the TV.

When I reviewed what happened, I realized that I felt lonely eating at the table by myself. It felt excruciating to make a dinner for one person while my person was in a war zone, so I sat in front of the TV to eat...and then never left. In my case, I had two next steps to take. The first was to make dinner plans regularly. The second was to find a therapist with whom I could discuss the feelings.

Every year around tax season, I notice that I

become inspired to clean anything and everything. I'll vacuum the silverware drawer, purge the spice cabinet, and oil my boots before sitting down to confront the reality of how much money I'll be paying Uncle Sam. It's an effective way to take full inventory of everything I own once a year, but it ends in shame and makes the process take a million times longer than it needs to.

In this case, I swapped the steps. Rather than procrastinating by cleaning, I would motivate myself to do increments of tax prep work 15 minutes at a time. I set a timer to attack the receipts and tally, then I spent 30 minutes cleaning or relaxing. In my case, I wasn't procrastinating by engaging in a negative behavior, just a distracting one. If your adorable coping mechanism is to stress shop, maybe consult your HC and find a better way to cope.

Lots of feelings here: inadequacy, embarrassment, and shame that I was unprepared for the taxes. Loads of old stories about money bubbled up and guess who I got to talk to about all of that? (My therapist.)

Gossip is a great behavior to look at because the definition of gossip is so nuanced. You've got to look at where, when, and with whom you're gossiping. If it isn't a problem for you, it isn't a problem. But say you keep burning bridges and find yourself friendless, which isn't where you hoped to be. You might notice that you gossip about things you're struggling with in your own life—someone *else's* money management problem, or drinking problem, or unwillingness to volunteer to host the next book club. Looking for these trends provides insight, because maybe it's just your unskillful way of sorting out your own problems.

Notice what you're gossiping about and then, instead of engaging, tell a safe person what you know. If you gossip and judge people's drinking, what do you think that's about? If you find yourself telling everyone how uninformed and uneducated the new board members are and how upset you are that they were selected, what does that indicate?

Maybe you are becoming aware of your relationship with alcohol in a way that feels uncomfortable. Maybe you're tired of serving on the board yourself or are insecure about how informed and educated you are on a particular subject.

Adorable.

Awareness is such a big part of this process, and any technique you employ afterwards is wonderful.

Interlude: Adulting

Everyone seems to have an opinion on my dating life these days. Things I should and shouldn't do on a first date or second date. What to wear. How long to wait afterwards to text or call. Whether no news is good news or simply another loose end. My relationship readiness in general. It's too much.

So I'm becoming an anthropologist of dating—a psychoanalyst. I'm learning so much about myself through this. First, that I'm an adult. Second, that adulthood is not in any way correlated with competency.

That's the lie of the driving age, the voting age, the drinking age. The idea that time in service equates some level of proficiency in making decisions. I have no idea what I'm doing.

The Greek Chorus of my friends and fellow wanderers seems to think I've got a few things going for me—that I'm smart and witty. Funny. Attractive. I've tried not to be. Dumbed myself down, chopped off my hair. It's easier to accept rejection when you're not playing at full volume—accept the outcome when it's just the flip of a coin. Harder when you're real, full force. Because then the rejection is real, fully earned. The biggest challenge is not believing it's deserved. That the rejection is more about cosmic forces in slightly—but significantly—different orbits.

See you again next life. Or not.

My therapist is trying to help me embrace the idea that I have needs that must be met by other people, that I'm not entirely self-sufficient and this is not, in fact, a sign of weakness. This is a sign of humanness. Humans are social and, even with my best cyborg impersonation, I am resigned to the fact that I am one. Part of being human is asking for help and asking again and again at different doorsteps, at different feet.

The biggest lesson to date, in the field of dating, is it takes a village.

My anxiety requires the assistance of 15 friends, a few yoga classes and a tribe of Al-Anoners to make sense of my disoriented position in the galaxy. And this is the gift—the realization that I have 15 friends. A yoga community. A room of people as twisted and as human as I am. We share the preoccupation with calibrating off the misguided signals of other people rather than our own screwed-up and perfect, molten cores.

I feel about 20 years behind at this, and pop culture offers no helpful dating tips. But neither are the opinions of a dozen people who are equally lost on this path. My solution—my resolution—is just to be me, fully, no holds barred. Less consideration for the "shoulds" and the "thou shalt nots," more respect for the inner compass. More willingness to say "help me" when I need it and "thanks for your opinion" when I don't.

Perhaps this is the mark of adulting.

FIVE

Four Types of Relationships

The single most useful boundaries teaching I ever received was from my former boss and teacher, Tommy Rosen. It was after I had worked for him for several years that I finally felt comfortable asking him a truly strange question.

"Tommy, you're an attractive man. I know this empirically. But I'm not attracted to you. Do you know why?"

"It's intentional," he replied.

This made no sense to me. How could my level of attraction to him have anything to do with his intention? Wasn't beauty in the eye of the beholder?

He explained that in the Sikh faith, there is an important teaching that everyone of the opposite gender must be treated as one of four types of relationships: parents, children, siblings, or partners. In that faith, you only treat one person as a partner. Everyone else you encounter must be treated as one of the others. You have an unlimited number of parents, children, and siblings, and in fact, one person might switch from one role to another in the course of a conversation. But you only have one partner.

"I'm not sending you partner energy," he said.

It changed the way I saw every single relationship in my life and reminded me that I get to decide how to behave in every circumstance. It was eye-opening, as I realized I had essentially one strategy in dealing with unsolicited partner energy: block and run.

I have always been in a romantic partnership. Since the age of 14, I could tell you who my other half was. In many ways, my behavior looks like that of a love addict because I was always partnered, but in other ways, I didn't fit that description at all. I wasn't obsessed with being partnered or dependent on my partner for my own sense of worth and place in the world. I was using my partners as a defense strategy.

It was an unskillful use of this concept that only one person can receive partner energy, and it made it so easy to say "no" to advances in coffee shops. Even in the (much later) years when I was single for the first time at 36, I would use a fake partner to deflect advances whether I was interested or not.

For example, if someone approached me at a coffee shop and I had any inclination they were hitting on me, I would shift the conversation to name drop my (imaginary) boyfriend.

"I do come here often! My boyfriend works right next door."

"Yes, I will pass the sugar. Also, my boyfriend likes sugar."

"Bless you. My boyfriend sneezes, too."

It was insane.

And? It was the best that I had to offer at the time. I borrowed the false boundary of my fake boyfriend to deflect even the possibility of an advance because I so desperately did not want to have to tell someone that I was single and, in my eyes, defenseless.

So much therapy followed.

In the ensuing years, I have learned that many other people employ this strategy for a variety of reasons. Others reciprocate flirting with flirting because it seems to be what is expected—you're traveling somewhere, someone in the airport says nice things to you, offers you a drink, and you're flirting back to be nice, or to continue the conversation, or for some other adorable reason.

This is exhausting and confusing because at some point you must either tell them you're not interested or sleep with them, at which point it will come out sideways that you're not interested. Or maybe you'll get married and 15 years later you'll finally get up the nerve.

It's easier to consider that you can reciprocate with energy that feels appropriate to you. Rather than reflecting partner energy, pretend that person is your sibling. You don't have to mention it in an overt way, just treat them like your sibling. You'll notice you speak differently, use different words, and even position your body differently when you are projecting sibling energy versus partner energy. This creates quite a lot of clarity and is often well received by the recipient as a soft "no thank you."

In other words, it voices your "green."

Your body posture, words, and affect can say "I'm open to sibling energy" without you having to say "I'm not open to partner energy," or blathering on about your real (or imagined) partner. It's really quite lovely.

Occasionally you might need to use the words. "Rennie, I'm open to sibling energy, not partner energy." They will get it. They may not like it, but it is so much clearer than the "friend zone" that we often use to describe this.

Try it out?

These relationship types can also be super helpful looking at your HC. Your higher council should be made of peers and mentors (siblings and parents). You should not have "children" types on your wheel—your HC members are there to be experts.

This does not mean that your children cannot advise you or be on your HC. Maybe you have a child who works in the theatre district, and you're trying to decide where to have dinner before a show. They are a great resource, and in that case, can act as a mentor/advisor because they have expertise. Even young children can be on your HC if you're looking to improve your Lego-building skills, your knowledge of the most recent superhero movie, or your proficiency at make believe. Children can possess skills and knowledge that you do not and can advise in these small ways.

Your young children should not serve as peers. They are not here to listen to you vent about your day at work, your spouse, or the patriarchy. If you find yourself nominating a child to that role, applaud your awareness and fill the seat with a more appropriate person who can offer a supportive ear more easily (and who has the gumption to say no if they don't have the space).

In the space of one conversation with a trusted friend, you might find yourself shapeshifting into all three roles. He asks you about your garden and you commiserate about the drought together (peer). Then he asks your advice about how to research skilled nursing facilities for his ailing mother (mentee). And then you talk about the new restaurant that opened by the river walk (peer). And then you ask him how he started dating after his divorce (mentor). This is a perfectly healthy conversation and follows the advice of staying within those three types of relationships.

In the space of a conversation with an elder in your faith or other wisdom tradition, you might ask a series of questions about the ethics of end-of-life care choices, the history of a particular teaching, and how you can financially support the bigger organization's efforts. In this conversation, you are being mentored, and you don't need to find a way to offer advice. You can find something peer-like to relate, and this is often what we call "small talk" because it involves relatively small shared experiences—things like the weather, a recent film, a news event, or a common friend. But you're unlikely to start offering them welding tips even if you're the savviest welder in all of the village because it would be weird. If they are a skillful mentor, they will offer an opportunity for you to mentor them in the same way skillful adults ask children to demonstrate their competence.

Interactions get weird when an "intimate partner" or sexual vibe is introduced when it is not shared, *and* the other person responds with vague energy. You get to feel romantic and introduce partner energy wherever and however you like, just prepare for some awesome consequences, maybe chat with your HC first, and remember that you can't decide what energy you will receive. If the receiving person is clear with their energy, then everything will be great no matter what—you will either enjoy some romantic time together or shift into a different zone without confusion.

When seeking a romantic partner, watch out for the unskillful "flirting back" without true interest, or the unskillful continued flirting in the face of sibling energy. While I cannot be certain this is what caused the Titanic to sink, this confusion has created so much chaos in so many lives that I wouldn't be surprised.

Caveats From the Patriarchy

In the Sikh faith, the classifications of parent, child, sibling, and partner are taught from a gendered and heterosexist perspective. Even so, I believe the theory still applies regardless of the genders of those involved in the exchange. In fact, even assuming heterosexuality as a default can still cause confusing relational dynamics! People who present themselves as heterosexual will still leverage sexual energy with individuals of their same sex; women leverage this in sales and recruitment all the time. I personally believe that many successful multi-level marketing schemes are profitable for women who are able to hetero-flirt others into their covens.

So, it is with this hetero-flirting argument in mind that I suggest we skip the analysis of these from a gendered lens and consider that all people of any gender can give and receive any of these four forms of energy. Wherever you and your compatriots land on the gender spectrum, the same rules apply.

Similarly, the Sikhs teach that all members of the opposite sex fall into the category of partner, child, parent, or sibling from a monogamist perspective. Monogamy is the assumed default of our culture even though we often behave differently. I'd like to amend this—I think it might be grand for each of us to consider what precisely we want in our relationships and then articulate it clearly in the dating process. I also think it would be lovely for us to allow and prepare for the possibility of graduation from a relationship, or of relationship closure. I suggest that if you consider yourself polyamorous or non-monogamous, you only present partner energy when that is your intent. While I believe those who are polyamorous or non-monogamous to be much, much more skillful at presenting their wants and needs clearly (because it is required in what society considers a non-default partnering pattern), it is helpful for those who are "considering" this option to know they retain their ability to be discriminate about where and how and to whom they present their energy. Being indiscriminately sexual or tossing partner energy about creates confusion and sometimes invites bizarre behavior, as it is often returned. It is sloppy and better options exist.

An incredibly common bastardization of this is the child-ification of one's partner. Many partnered couples slowly slide into siblinghood as their relationship relies less on sex and more on partnership, and then volleys back and forth between the two. Other partnered couples head in the direction of the Bermuda Triangle, seeking a pattern that is familiar in another way: one becomes the child, one becomes the parent, and it creates a dynamic that is not readily compatible with partner energy.

At the same time, certain sects of modern psychology tell us that we will seek out a partner who reminds us of conflict we had with a parent. While that might be true (and it's certainly worth discussing with your licensed mental health professional), it might also be strongly influenced by our cultural stories and sitcoms.

We often hear our friends complain about diminishing sex, lack of respect for household work, or lack of respect for out-of-household-work. We hear about marriages ending over recapping the toothpaste or rogue socks lying around, and to me, all of these sound like boundary challenges. Many of them feel like the parent/child relationship.

It may occasionally be acceptable for your partner to mentor you or for you to mentor your partner, but if this is a general trend, you may want to seek mentorship outside of the partnership. Even if your partner is a skilled personal trainer, it might not be appropriate for you to train with them if it feeds an unhealthy power disparity. You can see this clearly based on where you have placed them on your HC. They do belong there, likely in the inner circle and in certain sections, but not all sections—and likewise for you in theirs.

You shouldn't share the rest of your council members with your partner. Your HC and their HC might have some common folks, but hopefully there is significant variation in the middle circle. You might have the same doctor, accountant, and veterinarian, but the people you are texting for relationship advice should not be the same people.

Regardless of how we were parented, we do not want to be parented by our partners. Noticing ways in which you parent or behave like a child can help you reorient your relationship back into the partnership zone. And the support of some peers, mentors, and professionals can help.

Intimacy

We all want intimacy whether we know it or not, and how we go about getting it is really adorable. Some of us try to smother our people. Others play the "catch me if you can" method of taunting and running away. And still others are able to locate the "just right" zone of intimacy without effort. Those people are not reading this book (though neither are unicorns, for the record).

Intimacy is not exclusive to sexual or partnered relationships; it is something we can cultivate with friends, coworkers, family members, and others. It is an indication of closeness.

We often attempt intimacy through various unskillful methods—and maybe you'll recognize one or two of the methods you've employed below?

Rescuing and Being Rescued

Thank Disney for reinforcing the ridiculous idea that intimacy is forged when one person rescues another. Nearly every genre from romantic comedy to drama to tragedy rests a plot or subplot involving a romantic bond forged via rescuing—these include a prince saving a damsel in distress, a woman saving her falling-down-drunk friend/brother/father/partner from his battle with alcoholism. or one person physically or emotionally rehabilitating someone after a terrific accident, battle, or bout of depression. This formula of human interaction is so engrained in culture that psychologists have dubbed it the "victim triangle" or the "drama triangle." In this model, there is a victim, an aggressor, and a hero whose identity revolves around rescue.

We imprint off of this model because it is what we see and hear so often. I'm not sure many of us are aware of following this template unless someone from the outside looks in, or we repeat the pattern enough times with enough awareness to recognize it. Some people get stuck in a relationship they entered early in life rather than allowing a relationship pattern to gradually emerge—if you fall in love with your high school sweetheart and never date anyone else, how might you know what your tendencies are?

If you do some dating, you'll start to see if this is one of your adorable tendencies. Do you offer to pick up the check more often? Are you over-gifting? Do you rush to the rescue to bail your new significant other out of jail or other messes? Do you manage your expressions of emotion around their emotional states? If so, you're doing some rescuing.

I'm not interested in keeping score—sometimes we date in different tax brackets, and we also have friends at various levels of financial success, so it's not unreasonable for a more financially stable person to spend more money than a less stable person. I'm not suggesting a dollar-for-dollar tally; it's the trend and the motivation that matter. Your HC will be so helpful in identifying your trends, as will your observations of your past relationships for mirror-type behavior.

Escaping from the victim triangle requires you to

separate yourself from the need. The same applies here. You might notice that your person needs a new car. That does not mean that *you* need to buy them one, or research the purchase of one, or hotwire the next one you see outside the diner. A worthwhile question to ask yourself is, "Am I the best person to meet this need?" Then, run your response by a few folks on your HC to gather some team perspective.

Do you avoid paying for anything? Accept gifts that feel too good to be true? Do you feel that your affection is something you owe because of the other person's willingness to get you a job, buy you a house, or pay off your student loan debt? Do you find yourself leveraging your emotional meltdowns as a way of getting your way? Do you express your needs in a way designed to manipulate the outcome of different situations? If so, you're allowing yourself to be rescued.

Again, you need not keep score. It is perfectly lovely to receive support when it is needed, and many people do not do this well. You can choose to inventory yourself and determine whether you are always partnering or friending with people who meet your financial needs or bail you out of wild circumstances. Especially reflect back on anything you do that feels childish but not playful.

As with the victim triangle, remembering there are many places you can get your needs met will save you from victimhood. You can let the other person pay for you every single time, but does that allow them to buy the choice of where to go? Of what you eat? It can become a slippery slope. Finding creative and diverse ways to meet your needs can bust you out of the need to be rescued.

Trauma Bonding and Shared Hardship

One of my favorite episodes of *Dharma & Greg* (which I consider a sacred text of sorts) is one in which Dharma and Greg go to a couples retreat with both sets of their parents and do all the stereotypical relationship-strengthening activities—peeling potatoes, spending time in the rain, digging ditches. They all navigate it differently (and hilariously), and the shared hardship of the work does indeed strengthen their relationships.

It's an interesting idea to build intimacy by enduring challenges. I think it often works, but it's not a recipe for success unless there are tools. Both people need a counselor or support system to process their emotions and guide communication. Unprocessed resentment can fester and erode intimacy. I hear about it all the time.

People do not operate at their best when they are hungry or tired (or worst of all, both). When we endure these types of difficulties, we are operating at a lower level motivated by basic needs. Even if you and your beloved can endure a bad bout of the flu together in a home with one toilet, you will also probably say and hear some things you wish you hadn't. And while being willing to be seen in a vulnerable state is one thing that can create intimacy, acting like a jerk because you're dehydrated and missing the Red Hot Chili Peppers concert does not.

One variation of this adorable behavior is to select partners and friends who have a shared history of your version of trauma. It can be useful to have a community that understands and empathizes with trauma recovery, addiction, assault, or natural disaster, but be cautious that you don't surf in the dating pool or find all your friendships from that same angle. While it can be often ideal to partner with someone who doesn't drink alcohol if you're in recovery from alcohol, wonderful romances can still emerge in the most unlikely circumstances, and selecting exclusively from one group of people may prove a disservice. Ideally, those in recovery from addiction and trauma will grow beyond their initial trauma. Still, when trauma is the only glue holding a relationship together, many couples will choose their relationship over their own personal evolution and unconsciously decide to remain individually stuck.

For example, if the main topics of your conversations are about the deplorable living conditions you grew up in, or how awful it was to be raised by an addicted or neglectful parent, your conversations will stay small, circular, and negative. In some ways, this is the same as constantly talking about a shared red list. *Why the red list is red* is not the anchor of any healthy relationship. If you focus on growth and gratitude instead as many recovery programs encourage, you will benefit from limitless conversational possibilities and allow the "green" to grow and grow.

Gossip

Everyone gossips, even you. I catch myself falling back into unskillful patterns of gossiping all the time. Gossip serves an important social function by strengthening bonds of intimacy among the people who are gossiping at the expense of intimacy with the subjects of the gossip.

Humans are social, cultural beings who tend to live in limiting beliefs like "there is only so much room at the top" or "there are only so many seats at the table." When we're in a group, belonging is critical for our survival as none of us are qualified to live our days in full isolation. We want and need to be part of a social group that can check in on us when we are under the weather, or share in the rearing of our offspring, or pick up the newspaper while we're out of town.

When we gossip, we are defining the out-group and unskillfully defining the in-group by default. If Sally is in the out group because she is cheating on her husband, then we have accidentally defined the in-group as anyone who isn't cheating on their spouse. It's similar to answering a question like "where do you want to go to dinner?" with "anywhere but Taco Shack." You've defined that you don't want to associate with infidels and adulterers, and that's great —but define a green group rather than resting in the yellow land of "we may not like one another, but at least we're loyal."

Gossip is simply talking about red lines or

common red lists rather than focusing on the green. Once you realize this, shifting the conversation is so simple. Rather than railing against Sally for her adultery, criticizing her partners, making fun of her insecurities, or trying to guess whether or not her wife even knows, find the green. Ask your compatriots what they do to strengthen their relationships, how they have responded in moments of temptation or anything else in the green list. Let the conversation and group bonding work for you rather than circling the wagons around someone's scarlet letter.

Explore other topics you may have in common. Surely fidelity is not your only common thread. Look at your own green list to find conversations that light your fire and introduce new options to see where the puzzle pieces fit. This is why there are books and book clubs—they make for easy conversation starters and give us practice talking about subjects that aren't about other people.

Sex

I have no empirical evidence to support this but sex feels like a fast-forward button to intimacy—or maybe it's a fast-forward button only for some people and not for others. Wherever you fall on the spectrum, please be aware: sex is not the same for everyone. If you're in the camp of people who believe that sex equals long-term commitment, definitely say so before the pants come off, because not everyone agrees. That very confusion is the premise of countless adorable romantic comedies and is the root of a lot of heartbreak.

For some people, sex is a sign that they have "decided," and deciding to "make it work" with someone works—but only as long as the decision is *reciprocal*. Arranged marriages work partly because both parties agree that they will, and partly because those marriages are supported by a culture and family structure with built-in ways to manage their difficulties. One person deciding to make it work does not work. Ever.

If you start with sex, which I'm presuming is on the green list for you and your person, that's also unskillful, because it's important to discuss red list items first. If you can cover the red lists first, pants off —or if you and your partner agree on a short-term or defined-term thing and one of you is not in forever land, you also have my blessing.

Communities involved in kink and BDSM do an expert job of laying out rules of engagement for sex that heteronormative and vanilla communities often do not. Regardless of your sexual orientation and preferences, having a standard for communication is remarkably helpful. I believe this is why *Fifty Shades of Grey* was so popular—it isn't that all American women are sexually stifled or that everyone wants to be bound and gagged, it's that it introduced vanilla communities to sexual "rules of engagement." It had many faults, including poor writing, no plot development and ingrained misogyny, but it did suggest that what we want is okay and that other people have structure and tools that can benefit us, no matter what we want and need.

If you aren't familiar with some of the rules of engagement from other parts of the sexual spectrum, I'd love to introduce you to a few tools. None of my examples will involve specific acts—there are plenty of other books that do an excellent job of describing all possible plans of action. Rather, I'm going to break down the rules.

Terms of Engagement

Whether or not a relationship is monogamous requires a bit of conversation rather than simple avoidance and "hoping for the best." In communities that are not following a heteronormative template, exclusive relationships are often defined and described —which means the boundaries of the relationship have been consciously considered. Have you considered what monogamy means to you? Have you determined if it means precisely the same thing for you and your partner? What about if you are non-monogamous, where the same questions apply? What does your version of polyamory look like, and are the rules the same for you and your primary partner (if you choose to have a primary partner)? What is important for you to know about your sexual partners? What is important for them to know about you? While monogamy may seem like a simpler prospect (it certainly involves fewer variables), a lack of definition can cause strife in any kind of relationship.

Examples: "No harm in looking" might be true for one person (it's generally accepted as the standard), but is it true for the other person? Is looking different if it happens in person rather than online? Or through a window? Or if the looking is or isn't consensual?

"Talking isn't cheating" might feel true for one person in a relationship, but if someone is choosing not to disclose certain conversations for fear of arousing the other's jealousy, or if not disclosing is tied to feelings of shame or denial, is that assumed boundary around talking really true?

There are zero hard and fast rules about sex. Zero. Religious, governmental and recovery-oriented communities create their own rules of restriction. Other communities define rules of structure as well. I encourage you to consider your own.

What Works and What Doesn't

As I've previously outlined, secrets are usually an indicator that it's time to speak openly with a member of your HC. Exiting a relationship is often a fertile time to create scripts and protocols for what works for you and what does not. They don't need to be extensive, but if you frequently become bored by your partners and seek entertainment elsewhere, perhaps it's an opportunity to look at why and create protocols for yourself which (hopefully) involve telling your partner.

Fidelity by means of grin-and-bear-it is not intimacy. Healthy intimacy is fostered through voluntary vulnerability, like disclosing the fact that you are interested in someone at work or authentically sharing that your sexual interests and needs are evolving. There are professionals who specialize in facilitating these kinds of conversations, and I encourage you to enlist their services as they relate to cultivating intimacy through protocols (or find someone to keep on retainer).

Safe Words

In a world where painful or physically dangerous endeavors can be included in sexual practices, there is a protocol for saying "stop." I have not met a vanilla heterosexual couple that employs this emergency exit as a possibility. There is nothing magical about the word itself, but the contract it implies is crucial: you will define and uphold your own sexual boundaries and the other person will respect them; in turn, they will define and uphold their own and you will respect those as well. This level of open communication involves a huge amount of trust.

In the absence of physical danger, many people do not believe they have the right to say "no" or "stop," or else they believe their partner won't abide by their boundaries even if they do. You may even be one of these people going along with what you believe your partner or culture expects of you. I'm here to tell you that absolutely get to say "no" or "stop"—at any point, for any reason.

A Community of Fellows

If your "culture" consists solely of mentorship from the cast of *Friends*, you are on an island of illusory companionship. The same is true if all you ever do is ask yourself what Jesus or Oprah would do. If you have no one with whom you can discuss nuanced areas of your life, create a new section of your HC and prioritize filling those seats. Locate peers, mentors, and professionals who have some training and expertise—not a group of people who share your gripes.

Deal Breakers

Dan Savage has so much to say about healthy relationships—I love listening to and reading his wisdom because he's funny, insightful, and completely self-taught. As much as I adore academics, Savage came by his expertise honestly. Originally hired as a gay man offering sex advice for straight people in a newspaper humor column, he had the benefits of a unique cultural lens and the context of his non-normative experience. He quickly identified practices missing from straight relationships. Seeing things from outside of the default is an exercise in defining your own stance, perspective, and boundaries; the cost of fitting into what's "standard" is that we rarely have the awareness to do this for ourselves.

I think of Dan Savage as a bicultural being who walks between worlds, translating and offering the best of the outside to the inside (and maybe vice versa, though I'm not sure).

Many years ago, I found a clip of him offering a teaching that has become foundational to the boundaries process about the "price of admission." You can Google it and watch it for yourself, but the basic premise is he was replying to a woman who said she couldn't seem to locate a potential mate who didn't irk the crap out of her. She ended relationships quickly because her potentials didn't meet her standards, and she asked him how she would ever find someone who did.

His short answer was: she wouldn't.

He describes two lists: the deal breakers, of which you can have about five, and the price of admission. Deal breakers are his way of defining the red list and can be absolutely anything, but they cannot be *everything* or the entire dating pool will be swallowed. You'll waste your life dancing around the red line (and as he describes it, you'll end up alone with a sexrobot).

Everything else is the "price of admission," which I think of as the yellow list. He talks about his marriage and how his husband leaves the mayonnaise on the counter after making a sandwich; this is not a deal breaker, but it is the price of admission because Dan chooses not to let it be a source of argument. It isn't on his red list. He doesn't define his red list in the clip, but it took me many efforts to define mine, so I'm here to help you.

Brainstorm everything you have disliked about

partners. Make a big list, partner by partner or as they come to you. List all grievances big and small.

Never vacuumed. Taunted the neighbor's dog. Chewed with his mouth open. Was unreliable. Secretly smoked crack during Christmas dinner. Left the toilet seat up. Could not go to bed with dishes in the sink. Threw out perfectly good food. Wore socks two days in a row. Showered compulsively. Never wanted sex. Always wanted sex.

It should be cathartic.

Then, see if themes emerge.

Clean freak. Wasteful. Cruel. Demanding. Lazy.

You decide.

Then, see if you can create five categories for your red list. Be cautious not to include things that might land on the purple list as red list items—I noticed myself making this mistake when I started dating and my deal breaker list included:

- Not in active addiction
- Not a serial killer
- Not in another relationship with someone who thinks they are in a monogamous relationship
- Not a Gemini
- No bad teeth

I believe things like "active addiction" and "serial killer" are actually purple list items. They are so far outside the field of someone who is prepared to engage in a relationship that they are a given.

Depending on your preference for monogamy and non-monogamy, the part about relationships might also rightly land on the purple list. Have someone on your HC check your list and see if they think anything should be on the other side.

The great news for me is that I would drill my dates on the first date about all these qualities. If they found my list to be offensive or abhorrent, the date ended. Over time, the red list became more reasonable. Just like the other lists, red list items are personal preferences, not generally accepted societal norms.

- Active addiction became: no interest in self-improvement or work on the relationship.
- Serial killer became: lack of moral/ethical compass.
- Relationship deal became: unwilling to discuss/describe relationship needs, wants, desires, and preferences.
- No Geminis became: no Peter Pan Syndrome (excessively child-like and irresponsible behavior).

...and no bad teeth got folded into self-improvement.

If you have a history of relating with deplorable folks or dangerous relationships, maybe take some time off from dating (like a year). Please work with a therapist and find a program of support. Build a robust area for relationships on your HC and define your purple list first. Then get to work on the red list.

If you have a history of generally fine relationships not tainted with abuse, addiction, or criminal activity, just start with the red list and really work it. The end of one relationship is often the best time to do this work. Just like any area of your life, the only constant is change. Expect your red list to evolve over time and focus on expanding your green list.

The Truth, or Something Like It

People often come to me with relationship gripes, telling me things they have never said to their partner.

When I ask them why they haven't spoken to the person directly, they invariably say, "I don't know what to say."

After they have just told me 17 paragraphs-worth of detailed information. They aren't working through what is wrong; they are working through *how to relay it.*

I think we have been corrupted by the rules of a courtroom, where we are required to tell the truth, the whole truth, and nothing but the truth. It's a huge statement, very well crafted and refined, and it does not apply in day-to-day circumstances. I encourage people to state the truth or something like it.

Honesty is one of my favorite things, but the whole truth is often more than anyone can swallow. In a court of law, the truth is moderated by professionals who are not personally invested in the outcome of the conversation, so the whole truth is a worthy endeavor.

In the rest of the world, I don't need to know your whole truth, because it's likely to come with information that does not facilitate either intimacy or closure.

For example, you are upset with your neighbor because they let their dog poop on your lawn and don't always pick it up. You think it is gross. You feel disrespected. You spend several paragraphs detailing all their other annoying habits like their taste in lawn ornaments, their beat-up car, and how they leave the back light on all night. You mention that you think they smell, that they could use a fitness program, and that they sure buy a lot of cheese at Costco.

All of these things may be true, but if you simply open up to your neighbor with a list of grievances, several of which are valid and none of your damned business, you're likely to make your neighborly relations less joyful and more contentious. By venting and then processing with a peer or mentor, you can refine your list to the items that are your business, and then start a conversation that addresses your concerns.

I like to start by crafting a script. Usually it's just a starting line that begins with curiosity and can start a meta-conversation. A great opening line might be, "Hi Zelda, I'm wondering if you know that sometimes your dog poops on my lawn?" She may not be aware of it, in which case it is simple to say that you are seeing it and it crosses a boundary for you. Maybe your problem is that the dog is in your yard. Maybe the problem is that you're finding poop. Get clear and deliver the red/yellow/green of it.

If she replies that she is aware and that she isn't

going to do anything about it, you can end the conversation and return to your HC. You have identified and articulated your side and do not need to get all the way to resolution in one go.

And maybe she'll say something else, something that lets you into the reality of her life a bit more. Maybe she'll tell you something you couldn't have imagined, and you'll need to consider it further before you decide what your next step is.

In other cases, perhaps your grievance is something larger. You've been having an emotional affair and do not want to tell your partner, but you also feel that you need to tell them, because it is destroying your mental health and your ability to function in the world. The secret is gnawing at you and it needs to come out.

Kudos.

Find a therapist.

Also? Consult your HC and let the secret out to a trusted person first. I really do believe that a therapist is the right place to start because they are legally bound to keep your information private unless you are a danger to others. It's a safe place to disclose what is getting at you without worrying that the secret will make it back to your partner.

Once you and your therapist decide to share information, you can start with the meta-conversation. Rather than itemizing all the ways this person has met emotional needs for you or the ways you have neglected the needs of the relationship, you simply say:

"I have to tell you something that I don't want to tell you."

It's a great first line because it is true and because it contains no details. It lets you pass the conversation to them and they can give you a level of empathy. You've communicated the truth and, even if you cannot or choose not to share more details in the conversation, having an opening line can get you started.

Higher Council Scripts

I have also found it helpful when serving in a mentoring role to have some scripted replies for circumstances that might trigger or impact me. Even though you're not engaging in a therapeutic role as a mentor in the HC, coming up with a deck of scripts can serve you in responding rather than reacting and can give you time to process information.

"I'm So Glad You're Here."

This is my go-to one liner. I practice it every time people come to my yoga class because it is always true. Whether they are coming just to practice or to tell me they are newly pregnant, their cat just died, they just lost a job, or got a divorce, the answer is still the same. I'm glad they are there.

Then, I pause.

Maybe they want to say more. Maybe they don't. Pausing after stating my truth lets them decide. They often proceed into class without saying more. Occasionally, they want to share more. I listen and then usually follow with another scripted line.

I started doing this because I saw yoga teachers taking on so much more responsibility for their clients than the scope of their practice. The scope of a yoga teacher varies from location to location and lineage to lineage, but they are still beholden to the laws of the land and, unless otherwise credentialed, are not therapists or medical providers; they teach a mixture of philosophy and movement. The balance between the two can be delicate at times, because philosophy has some good advice as well.

Higher council, baby.

"That Must Be Hard."

My follow up line is often "that must be hard." I don't apologize unless the thing that has upset them is my fault (and it rarely is), but I do hear that it is hard. I also don't counter with my own personal experience unless they ask for it. Telling them about what I did when my cat died is unhelpful. As is my divorce. And anything else. Even when they ask about it, I may not answer with my own personal experience, but with some form of philosophy or referral.

"My divorce was different, but I found that working with a couples' therapist was helpful in navigating the process," or, "yoga has some interesting ideas as it relates to the cycle of life and death, if you're interested."

"There Are No Words for This."

And sometimes, there just aren't words. Nothing you can say will spontaneously heal a loved one, repair a relationship, or bring someone back from the dead. When someone loses a family member or close friend, there are no words. So that's what I say. And sometimes, "There are no words for this. If there is something you want me to say right now, please let me know, otherwise I'm just here."

You may find that your life requires different scripts for circumstances, or maybe some ways to say "that's not my job" or "I don't want to share that with you."

I lean on humor (if you hadn't noticed), and most often it is well received. Occasionally, I am admonished for my sarcasm, and I accept that. It's adorable, and I'm not ready to put it down quite yet.

I have worked with some members of my HC to come up with reasonable scripts to acknowledge rather than respond when someone brings up a topic I find triggering. This is a much better strategy than faking a seizure, which was my previous strategy, and faking a seizure is better than snarling, which is my unfiltered and most authentic reaction.

Infertility, divorce, and conversations around gun safety laws all amp me up and get me into fight-or-flight mode within seconds. And yet, infertility and marital status are very common (and unskillful) topics people rely on to cultivate intimacy with strangers or to create "small talk," so they come up frequently.

My HC has helped me craft the following responses to scenarios that trigger me. It has helped me to feel less triggered, so I don't need to use the scripts unless I feel reactive.

Question: "When are you planning to have children?"
Response: "2012."

This is helpful because it says the whole answer in one simple statement. It's been awhile, and it clearly hasn't happened.

Question: "You've been dating for quite a while now. When is he going to pop the question?"
Response: "I have a strict policy that we must date for 40 years before we even discuss getting married."

It's funny, and it's true. I know that marriage is the right choice for many people, for lots of reasons. I also know marriage is not the right choice for many people who decide to go forward anyway because they think it is the "right" thing to do. Is that you? If so, I'm so glad you're reading my boundaries book. For me, dating for 40 years is my personal green because, at that point, I believe I will have confidence in the marriage lasting for the rest of my life.

Question: "Are you two married?"
Response: "Not to each other."

Again, I hope it is funny. It is true, we are not married to one another, and we're not married to other people either (I am pretty sure). I hope it is a kind way of ending a conversation rather than having to explain why we're not married, why I don't want to get married again, and how much I will not discuss "why we don't just adopt" with a stranger. And if you're curious, "just" adopting is as easy as "just" climbing Mt. Everest. It is totally possible, many people do it, and it requires a heap of training, paperwork, heartache, and effort on the front end.

Your scripts do not need to be funny or clever. They should feel natural to you and summarize a first statement so that you can get your feet beneath you and then either continue the conversation with a full breath or run away.

Which is always an acceptable option.

If no one has ever told you, you are always permitted to take space at any time for any reason. Your response can be a one-line closer before you exit the conversation.

"I hear my mother calling." Exit.

"I need to take my medicine." Exit.

"I have to end this conversation." Exit.

Onward.

Interlude: Rhizomes

The tenth wedding anniversary is aluminum or tin—to demon-
strate how a successful union requires flexibility and strength.
I'm writing this bit on my tenth. Do I still get to count it, even
if there is a pesky divorce in the middle?

I'm counting it.

Despite his hiatus from technology and texting, precipitated
by his sordid and confusing love life (which does not include
me), he texted me this morning, just after I took my computer
outside and wrote a blog post about being divorced on this
anniversary:

"Ben is getting ready to go to India for the next five months,
to study Tibetan in an immersion school. I feel so good about
this.

Yes, I thought. This *is your path.* This *is part of why we*
separated—so you could go, and I could love you for it rather
than resenting you for it.

I got to see him for a few hours and chat about the impor-
tant things. Share feelings in a way I haven't been able to share

105

with anyone else because he knows me in a certain way that no one else does.

I find it interesting that we describe separation as part of divorce—it is what you do before you divorce. Then the judge and the notary are supposed to shove their gavels and stamps between the sides and create a clear separation.

But I don't feel that separation. I feel roots.

When we got married, I carried a bouquet of golden aspen leaves. Our people wore aspen pendants and corsages, and we ate aspen-shaped chocolates. It's weird, I suppose because the leaves aren't flowers and it wasn't traditional. But it was authentic and it has deeper meaning for me now.

Aspen trees are rhizomes—one root system lives for thousands of years, sending up various trees whose individual life spans are short among the chorus of their neighbors.

Each tree contributes to the colony, investing its life into the roots. What we see as independent trees is simply an illusion.

How's that for poetry?

As I once wrote, some marriages fail without ending, and I believe ours ended without failing. I believe we poured our life-force into the roots, and we are each better for it. And while we may not be walking hand in hand in this life, tethered by rings and official documents, our connection persists.

The separation you see, is simply an illusion.

I locked it up and he texted,

'Happy Anniversary. I love you.'

It made me cry, but not for sadness, for joy at being remembered. For me, the tenth anniversary is clean. Shiny.

Tin seems about right.

SIX

Bingo

One of the most useful tools I've ever encountered was created by Martha Beck, who is an inspiring and joyful writer with more professional education and personal experience than should rightly fit into one person. She introduced me to the idea of "dysfunctional family bingo" which I have adapted and expanded upon here (while removing the *dysfunction* and the *family*).

Her basic premise was that prior to spending time with family for the holidays, one might sit down and create a bingo board outlining all of the typical ways family members can irritate you. Your uncle who steers all conversations in the direction of his pet master's degree in psychology, your sister who maintains an invisible six-foot leash on your niece with her gaze and constant hovering, or your grandmother who always tells the same story about the year someone exploded the Christmas turkey through the pressure cooker's emergency release valve and everyone ate fish sticks from the freezer instead. Maybe you have a creepy neighbor that gives you a sick-ish feeling, or you crumble into a puddle of tears when someone brings up your weight or diet suggestions. These are the crucial aspects of the bingo card because it gets it all out on the table (board).

I love this tool, because I love the idea of predicting the adorable behaviors and dysfunctions that can happen in a known environment. It helps to shift perspective from everything that could go wrong to how adorable everyone is and how smart you are for anticipating their weirdness. Rather than getting irritated that your dad is sneaking his broccoli to the dog during dinner, you can be slightly amused.

In the years when I co-owned a prenatal/post-partum yoga studio, I would suggest this to new blended families as an ideal way to prepare for the integration of a new baby into a family of in-laws (or outlaws), by encouraging my mamas to sit down with their partners and create a bingo card of what to expect based on the family they were going to visit. This was an opportunity for one side to brief the other on the possible weirdness they might encounter. It cultivated intimacy by exploring the sorts of behavior the partner found adorable, irritating, and intolerable in their family.

I then suggested that they select the few intolerable (red) items and make plans (scripts) for managing them if they arose.

- Adorable: Dad and broccoli, Grandma and retelling the tired fish stick story
- Irritating: sister's hypervigilance, uncle's self-absorption
- Intolerable: neighbor near children, conversations about weight and diet

Now, you and your partner can simply laugh off the broccoli scenario (or even watch for it!), redirect or close irritating conversations and make a plan for the intolerable. Maybe you decide to address the neighbor scenario with the hosts and ask them to invite the neighbor to another party, or maybe you make a plan to run an errand as they come over, removing yourself from the conversation and holing up at a coffee shop, yoga class, or library. And for the weight conversation, the other partner can have a script ready to go. *This is your moment!*

"Beulah, I'm sorry to interrupt you, but Chris is not open to conversations about weight this Hanukkah."

Boom.

You might also create code words with your partner to indicate that something has transpired and you need to close the conversation very quickly. It should be a unique word that others are unlikely to drop into conversation that your partner can listen for. My favorite word is Switzerland.

"Did you read that article about the new art exhibit from *Switzerland*?"

"Tim, did your sister return from *Switzerland* yet?"

"One of my coworkers brought me this incredible chocolate from *Switzerland* this year, and what you have here really reminds me of it!"

Now the partner launches into action with the plan. Maybe the plan involves blatant honesty ("we're not talking about weight") or closure ("I'm really feeling the need for a nap—can we head to the hotel soon?"). But it relieves the close family member of having to forge and enforce boundaries solo.

This scenario works well for cocktail parties, work engagements, family occasions and more. And better than that? It creates intimacy between partners who must anticipate and then discuss things they find triggering. It's overwhelming to visit the in-laws and try to volley every minor irritation—this usually leaves an exhausted partner and a family who thinks your partner is unfriendly. Or, more commonly, the partner feels paralyzed and not empowered to step in, so they simply watch the melee and grit their teeth.

I believe that honesty is a very good policy and that some of these strategies will support you in being fully honest with your family. They pave the pathway to full honesty and transparency. More importantly? They help you be fully honest with yourself and learn to embrace the idiosyncrasies that you find adorable. Maybe one day you'll even find yourself recounting the story of the liquified turkey on the ceiling and the fish sticks that saved the day.

This strategy is ideal for partners heading into a family gathering but can also be adapted for other uses.

Family Vacation Bingo

If your family is heading on a trip, creating a family bingo card can help to alleviate travel stress—and you can work through it with verbal children. Littles can watch and observe, and school-aged children can help anticipate breakdowns and solutions as well. For example, say your blended family of two parents, a 14-year-old, an eight-year-old, and a toddler are all traveling internationally to attend a conference where you are presenting and do a little sightseeing. You've traveled by airplane as a group before but never internationally.

The four of you sit down to create your travel bingo card and you find the following items:

- Slight delay leads to insufficient diaper changes for the baby, requiring a beg/borrow/steal approach from other parents.
- The ever-curious, wandering eight-year-old wanders away from the family once through security, causing both parents premature grey hair.
- The airplane announcements are loud!
- Tablets are to be powered down during

takeoff and landing, the most vulnerable times for a two-year-old.

- Luggage lost and delivered six days into the trip. Everyone wears clothing purchased at a thrift store (laundered).
- Hotel soaps are free, mini-bar snacks are not.
- Weather is unpredictable.
- Moving walkways are particularly entertaining for four out of five family members.

Then, you sort these by circling those that require a strategy (or are intolerable):

- Buddy system for child wandering
- Contingency diapers as a back-up plan

Those that are irritating:

- Diversify your luggage among many bags (in case it gets lost)
- Plan to distract the baby during takeoff and landing

And those that are adorable:

- The weather
- The minibar
- The moving walkway

How you address your own bingo card is completely up to your family. Maybe you go von Trapp and all wear matching Where's Waldo shirts in the airport for easier spotting. Maybe you implement a buddy system for wandering. Maybe you tether the toddler to an adult and insist on hand-holding. So many creative possibilities, and if you discuss them as a family, you facilitate intimacy by learning what is interesting and important to the other members.

Irritations can be mitigated in the same way if necessary, but they likely require less buy-in. Novel, quiet toys and books are great ways to anticipate battery-free time, as are special snacks reserved only for emergency scenarios. Maybe you decide as a family not to check a bag and instead make the thrift shopping and laundromat time a part of the travel experience. Maybe you diversify the luggage and have one outfit for each person in each bag. It can be so fun.

And the adorable things? Bring earplugs for the loud announcements, snacks for everyone, and look out for weather-related souvenirs like umbrellas, sun hats, and mittens.

Redux

The great thing about bingo is that you can employ it both before *and* after the occasion or trip. The first time you bring your new baby to the in-laws, you might anticipate certain weirdness. Maybe they suggest you "drug your baby to sleep" or chide you for keeping your little one too close or too far at all times. You can then revisit bingo while the recent engagement is close in your mind and get ready for the next family feud.

After the trip, you will learn about new possible snafus and can create a library of tools (and tales) of how your family manages when lost in Brussels with the wrong currency and no common language—or when the airline has cleverly re-seated the eight-year-old at the other end of the plane.

God Box

At the end of every yoga class is an opportunity for release—*savasana*. This practice is one of disintegration, as the work you have done reintegrates. It is release from attachment and full surrender. It is also a practice. I usually end my classes by saying "if surrender comes easily, go," by which I mean there are times you are ready to release something and it floats effortlessly away from you. Other times, you will need to practice through techniques like focusing on your breath or the floor beneath you, or scanning the body for residual tension before surrender becomes possible. Even with these techniques, there are days when surrender does not happen and you simply lay quietly waiting for class to end.

I love control in a way I had never truly understood until I entered the world of recovery. Prior to recovery, I would often describe myself as an "addict without a vice," and would expand by saying that I didn't like to lose control, so drinking or using mind-altering substances was never of interest to me. In some ways, you could say that control was my addiction—vigilance turned to hypervigilance, and I was wound tighter than any spring, ready to jump into action. My plans had plans and my lists had lists, and I didn't see anything wrong with it.

I was also miserable.

My love for structure and rules made me quite capable of predicting the behavior of others—it lured me into a realm where I would practice my capacity for being in control by baking six things at once, planning out the wet and dry measurements in the most precise manner. I stage-managed plays and performances on the side, opportunities to practice honing my illusion of control, and it was just these sorts of activities that helped me hide from my own pain and complete lack of control over certain people in my life, aspects of my body, and weather patterns.

You have likely heard the Serenity Prayer whether you've ever attended a 12-step meeting or not. It's lovely and simple and provides some important guidance:

> *God, grant me the serenity*
>> *To accept the things I cannot change*
>> *To change the things I cannot accept*
>> *And the wisdom to know the difference*

The prayer is in beautiful synchronicity with the teaching of yoga that discernment is a useful skill, but its cousin judgement is less so. I believe that judgement is on the path to discernment and can be used to identify your "wisdom to know the difference." Then you can either accept or change and it's your choice.

Changing is my mode of preference. I'll push through almost any challenge because I don't like to ask for help and because there is an adorable part of me that still thinks I have something to prove. It's there, and sometimes, it says hello.

The acceptance part was new to me.

Should we not be making lemonade out of the lemons life hands us? This requires effort. Who is just sitting around with a lap full of lemons saying, "Thanks, I'll just accept this remarkable sourness?"

No one. But maybe someone is sitting around thinking, "I can just let these lemons be lemons. I don't need lemonade. I can just accept that I'm perfectly okay right now and hold still in the presence of lemons."

People may not be saying that either, but it's the point I'm trying to make.

In the rooms of recovery, people talk about the "God box." Some people make legitimate boxes—with fully decorated folded paper or something purchased at an antique store—where things that are deemed "outside of my control" are offered. You write them down:

"My neighbor's taste in lawn ornaments."

"North Korea."

"My cousin's drinking."

The little slips of paper go in the God box. The act of writing it down, deciding to let it go, and then feeding it to the box is quite useful. Especially for those of us who prefer to effort our way to exhaustion, solving other people's problems and poking our noses where they do not belong.

In addition to *savasana*, yoga has another way of making this tangible—using a fire puja. Depending on lineage and custom, you might take grains of rice and repeat a mantra, offering the rice to a special fire. My experience of this is that it is as liberating as the God box and better done in the full ceremony of an appropriate guide or host. You're unlikely to find this at your neighborhood yoga studio, but should you find yourself in an ashram, give it a go. It's quite liberating.

In homage to the God box, I have used it to frame quick check-ins with peers on my HC (and sometimes mentors). We might briefly share "God box and wins," meaning: "What are we surrendering and what are we celebrating?"

If I were to do this today, I would place the local yoga studio's schedule in the God box, as it never seems to fit my needs, and I like to blame it for being so inconsiderate. I would also add my internet service provider, who has been intermittently disconnecting and reconnecting my service for the last few weeks apparently on a whim, despite the fact I'm paying what they have asked.

And my wins? I did a bit of writing earlier this morning, I said no when I meant no, and I received excellent feedback from two clients who responded to me asserting my needs and wants by sharing theirs calmly and diplomatically.

It's a super easy way to start or end a check-in with your therapist, your sponsor, your clergy person, or your HC person. "God box and wins" will open up conversation about what you've been experiencing since your last check-in or, at minimum, will leave you on a high note.

In my life, I have made the formal and executive decision to count all wins.

You're welcome to count your wins too.

Best Defense: Not Be There

The blockbuster '80s movie *The Karate Kid* had a greater influence on my upbringing than I'd like to admit. It was an inspiring underdog story about a puny kid getting strong, opening his cultural mindset, and embracing an Eastern art. There are so many gold nuggets in this movie, and I encourage you to connect with it again and see how many gems you can uncover.

The most salient point?

"Best defense: not be there," says Mr. Miyagi.

Some circumstances are really uncomfortable and mostly unavoidable—the DMV, the hospital, the post office, testifying in court. In truth, one can avoid all of them, but the consequences are potentially even worse than participating. If you decide not to drive, you don't have to go to the DMV. You can choose to work with your illness or injury outside of a hospital. You can hire someone to manage your post office needs and you can refuse to testify—although you'll likely be detained and lose more choices by doing that.

Other irritating circumstances can be avoided. A great teaching of yoga is that "the suffering which has not come can be avoided," meaning, you can always make a different choice. If you dislike crowds, you don't have to attend the Super Bowl ever again. If you don't like waiting in line, you can make strategies to avoid post offices and banks during peak times or use other routes to access those services.

Over time, I have identified circumstances that, for me, are not worth the effort they require:

- Weddings and associated parties (bachelorette, bridal showers)
- Baby events (baby showers, birthday parties)
- Almost all events hosted at bars

I did my due diligence, making my red/yel-low/green about weddings and the associated parties, and learned that there isn't much green. You basically have to pay me and give me an explicit role. You can hire me to play the violin at your wedding or manage the event flow, but I am unable to perform the cere-mony, stand up as a matron, of do any sort of mingling.

I made a wedding bingo card recently, as I was prepping to attend the wedding of my partner's best friend. Ninety percent of the squares contained things that were intolerable or irritating, although none of them were associated with the personalities I would encounter at this *particular* wedding. It included:

- Wedding toasts about everlasting love
- Tips about staying together forever
- Turning to a neighbor and sharing something from the heart
- The inequality of male and female roles in a traditional wedding
- Whorish makeup
- Single-use clothing
- Imported flowers
- Gendered attendant roles
- Bachelor parties
- Bachelorette parties
- Drinking
- Cigars
- Uncomfortable shoes
- Casual conversation about my life plans
- Casual conversation about what I do for a living

This list is good evidence that I'm not ready to go to a wedding. Maybe at another point in my life or when contained within the items of my green list, I might consider attending. This time, I did anyway based on my "get out of jail free" policy.

I will go to one wedding. Ever. Is this the one you choose?

I will. And I will hold in all of my emotions as best I can.

Which I did. I don't think I said much that was offensive, except possibly that I met my partner at a strip club and that very few people knew he worked as a stripper. It isn't true, and it also isn't a funny joke in some circles.

I also suffered heatstroke.

My efforts to ignore the uncomfortable feelings in my body were so extreme that I was not aware I was thirsty and overheating. The sickness got me out of a good portion of the reception, and after the sun went down, I made another appearance and learned that my heat stroke was the talk of the party.

What happens when you cross the red line?

It has a cost.

My experience of baby showers and parties is essentially the same. I am very good when I have an explicit role—helping soothe a mother during child-birth is where I shine because I've been trained to read all of her non-verbal cues and to translate them. I can easily escape to a place of control. Even though no one is able to control a birth, I can offer a sense of calm and steadiness and become the eye of the hurri-cane. I do not have the same capacity at baby showers and birthday parties.

I made an exception when my best friend's twins turned five this past year. I agreed to make an appear-ance at the party. I had a plan and specific objectives: I would stay for at least 15 minutes. I would connect with each twin, say happy birthday, and offer a hug. I would hug my BFF. I would call two friends on my way out.

Despite the fact that we are best friends, we don't have a common friend group. The people at the party were the parents of her children's friends. This left me in a remarkably uncomfortable and surprising circumstance: all adults introduced themselves to me by asking, "So which kid is yours?"

It was a very reasonable question to ask at a kids' birthday party, but also the worst possible question to ask me. None of my scripts worked.

"I'm glad you're here."
    "That must be hard."
    "There are no words for this."

Technically, the third script works, but I couldn't even muster it because of the shock. Each time, I turned on my heels and went to the buffet.

I saw the twins. I lasted my 15 minutes. I left without saying goodbye because I was choking back the uncontrollable tears that come when you've been surprised by your worst, triggering nightmare.

I played out a variety of replies like "I don't have kids" or "I'm their mom's best friend" or "I'm infertile," but couldn't manage them. At this point I cannot manage saying these things out loud, and I cannot handle the possible reply of "what kind of weirdo comes to a child's birthday party without kids?" I'm confident no one would have said it except the gremlins in my own mind.

My poor friends, who scooped me up afterwards and helped me return to sound enough mind to drive away, will attest—I am not ready for this stuff.

And I may never be.

I choose to celebrate birthdays in my own way out of self-preservation. I'd be happy to take the boys out to their own celebration. I'm happy to mail them a gift.

If you have situations in your life like this, consult your HC and see if it's possible to make a plan. Use the tools together: red/yellow/green, higher council, and bingo, and create a roadmap of what is possible. Understand the potential pitfalls, backup plans, and costs associated. Then do your best.

And remember. Sometimes the best defense is not to be there.

Motivation Wheel

Some of us are driven by the excuse machine. At some point we were rewarded for coming up with creative excuses and are so adept that we sometimes fool ourselves.

Our motivation is always multifaceted.

We have public reasons, which may or may not be related to the truth; personal reasons, or the reasons we tell ourselves; and then real reasons. Sometimes, all reasons point to the same decision. Other times, there is dissonance and confusion between our internal and external motivations.

Other self-help books will tell you to go with your

inner wisdom vs. the public reason. I'm not the sort of person to tell you which is better—remember, it depends. For instance, if you have a tendency driving the internal motivation (like addiction, or a preference for something criminal), going with your internal motivation or gut instinct is *not the best choice*. Sometimes cultural norms are more useful guides than internal motivations.

Case in point: I love coffee so very much. It's delicious. I love brewing it, the taste, the ceremony, everything about it. And? It does not improve my health. It drains my chi, causes anxiety, and makes me more susceptible to the voices in my head that tell me I'm not good enough. I can skillfully make arguments both for and against coffee on all levels. The truth is both that I love the taste and ritual, and it does not improve my mental health or functioning.

Should I drink it?

When I find myself in a draw or uncertain of my own motivations, I like to leverage the wheel of motivation. I brainstorm as many reasons as I can conceive of that could be motivating me and then chart them on the graph (see image). Then, I grade the level of intensity with which I currently experience each truth:

- Taste
- Ritual
- Habit
- Sociability
- Warmth

- Mental boost
- Obstinance
- Antioxidants
- Scientific proof that it's sometimes good

I try to get to 12. In the above example, taste, warmth, and mental boost all rise to the top of most true in the moment, which is so excellent. It means I'm looking for something that I like the taste of, something warm and something that will support my mental performance.

I could do this with decaf coffee. Green tea. A bit of chocolate and a nap. There are many more options now that I'm specific and not trying to just make my case for coffee.

Another example: I want to go to San Francisco to see my favorite band, but I'm having a hard time feeling completely good about the decision. I wonder what else is playing into this:

- Favorite band
- Flowers
- Meet an airline mileage program milestone
- See my friend
- See my ex-boyfriend
- Take a train
- Avoid a wedding
- Avoid saying no to the wedding

Ah. As you might guess, I'm willing to spend

$3,000 and five days of my life to avoid something, and I'm using my band and the other mini-reasons as excuses. All of the motivations are true in this case— they are just different levels of true. If I map it out and see that I'm most strongly making this choice to avoid having to either say no to a friend or attend his wedding, I can brainstorm many other wonderful ways to get out of the wedding—like telling the truth! Or picking up a contract job. Or feigning illness. Or driving to a mountain cabin that will cost me a tenth of the money and time and offer the same excuse.

Obviously, I need to contact my HC and figure out how to either decline the wedding invitation or make peace with going. I can red/yellow/green the attendance and make a bingo card, and if I still feel strongly averse, I'll create a script. It will say, "I love you, and I'm not allowing myself to attend weddings right now, for the safety of everyone involved."

Or I can fly head-first into some credit card debt and the drama of my ex-boyfriend—also effective, but probably without a single yay vote from any of my HC folks.

Why This is Better Than Pro and Con

Lots of people make lists of pros and cons. I love this because I love listing. Making lists calms me down, and I love it almost more than anything else in the world (except coffee). I'm so good at it and I'm so creative that I can make a tremendously compelling "pro" list and then hastily create the "con" list. Or vice versa, as my internal compass suggests. Because I'm also very smart, if I were to present this list to my therapist or HC member, they may not see through my adorable tendency to stack the deck in my own favor and encourage me to work harder on the "con" list.

You are completely welcome to lie to yourself using the motivation wheel, but you might as well stop reading and just burn this book. If you're in it to unpack the "whys" of your motivation, this will give you at least 12. Then, as you present them to your HC, it will provide wonderful conversation starters and help reveal your innermost truth.

So, your old boyfriend lives there, eh? How do you suppose being in the same city is likely to unfold? Are you planning to get together? Are you planning to stay at the hotel right across from his house? Are you planning to get breakfast at his regular coffee shop?

It goes much deeper than pros and cons.

Costs and Benefits

Again, I love lists. If you'd like to sit down and make lists of costs and benefits of your decisions, I support you in doing this. It is different from what motivates you. What motivates you is what you focus on first, then you look at the costs and benefits. (Oh, look! I'm willing to take the $3,000 solution that lands me in a wasp nest of old drama.)

Evaluating the costs of doing something may reveal useful information, but it won't be nearly as useful as uncovering your true motivations for doing it. You can fool yourself over and over this way but hopefully, with the right team members on your HC, you'll have the opportunity to make new and different mistakes rather than repeating old ones.

Causes of Suffering

Yoga teaches there are several causes of suffering and each makes an appearance on your wheel at some point. The two most common are craving and aversion, but we can just take a quick peek at all of them to identify the sources of your suffering.

Ignorance

If you don't know any better, it's hard to do any better. Ignorance is defeated in the process of making the wheel when you uncover that you do know what you are doing. You can then choose to do it anyway, but you will no longer not know. You'll be doing it consciously, and bravo to you.

Ego

Everyone has their way of understanding the ego, so for the sake of the motivation wheel, we'll call it blind selfishness instead. Some people refer to this as the obstinate child or the basest function. I actually love this one so much that I have labeled it adorable. Our adorable egos are often so repressed in other areas of our lives that they take hold and step forward when no one is looking. They eat the last cookie, or cut in line, or make an intentional dent or scratch in a refrigerator they're about to buy (because they know they'll get a discount if they do).

Craving

This is the big one for so many of us. We experience intense craving for connection, for time, for chocolate. When we give in to the craving, we often feel satiated for a little while before feeling ashamed and unfulfilled. Or maybe we're just disappointed, because the craving itself was much more intense than the relief of fulfilling it.

If you apply this to the motivation wheel, you can see a couple of cravings: meeting the airline mileage status level and seeing the ex-boyfriend. Neither one will offer lasting happiness, and both are likely going to lead to my being disgruntled or ashamed.

For some people, seeing a favorite band is a craving state—you're trying to reenact some previous experience. You'll know if it is a pattern for you. Do you usually go to concerts, enjoy yourself, and then immediately plan the next one without letting the enjoyment of this one sink in? Do you reach for a second or tenth cookie, or pull the lever on the slot machine again, or check Instagram one more time just in case this is the time the craving is satiated?

Aversion

My favorite place to play is aversion. While craving folks tend to think, "what could go wrong—it's just a cookie?!", I have a comprehensive list and plans for all the things that could go wrong. I want to avoid a wedding and I want to avoid telling someone that I want to avoid their wedding. Running away from people, actions, or possibilities qualifies as aversion. Its result is worse than a missed wedding—it leads to a very small life of not leaving the house or never trying anything new.

People die when they leave the house, don't you know?

I am very good at hiding my aversion with other, more rational reasons. The underlying truth is that the one or two reasons that fall into this category are what I look for when getting to the bottom of my motivation. Notice that these aren't any more *real* than the other reasons; they are all real reasons, they are just more intense and more in line with my tendencies.

Fear of Death

People also die at home (I have to remind myself), and fear of death is the final cause of suffering. It used to motivate me more than I'd like to admit. From childhood, I've been keenly aware that my parents will not live forever. I used to spend time with them because *what if this is our last Christmas together?* It was insane, and I mean that in the literal sense. No one wants to spend time with you because they are afraid that this is their last chance and no, it doesn't make everything better. So far, I have not been motivated by my own mortality in a real way, although I do contemplate it every time I consider going into debt to have an experience.

Adorable.

Knowing my tendencies, it's important for my HC folks to help me investigate if I'm driving all the way to visit my parents because I'm afraid they won't be there for a subsequent visit or because I truly want to spend time with them.

Interlude: Hunter's Blind

Woke up this Christmas in the Hunter's Blind. Despite her access to an overabundance of the world's resources, my mother bought this camouflage bedding for the room that was once mine.

It is hideous. Which is a fact.

And it is an example of my mother doing her best to take care of me, which is what mothers tend to do. Once we're too big to pick up by our scruff, or to put down in a laundry basket or manger for a minute, shit gets too complicated, our expressions of love colored by unintended consequences of our behaviors, the stars, and reactivity.

My meditation this morning was at someone else's altar. Wood, grown and carved in Africa, the deities faceless yet iconic in context. Donkeys. Sheep. Primitive doulas. Peaceful bovids gathered protectively around the place where God sleeps.

As a child, my attention would always float to the angel, whose presence was the only thing that let you know that this birth was different. I was also concerned that the sticky tack holding her to the lean-to was going to drop her right into the face of God. So there was that.

(Worry is my own mother's flavor of love, and so I suppose that's fitting, too.)

This morning my eyes rested on Joseph, the unsung hero of the virgin birth. The neo-feminist in me has always appreciated the sacrifice, the devotion, the efforts of Mary, whose body was hijacked and used as a vessel. I'd love to hear her reports of the story of this immaculate conception, but unfortunately hers was not a speaking role.

But Joseph? He showed up. The faceless man in front of me still went to Bethlehem, bent over another man's child, and stepped in. Eventually shared his gifts of carpentry, craft as a good way of expressing love. To show up, share your gifts, and wait for the Wise Men to come and give you some tips on your next move.

It's fitting, if you ask me, that neither of these parents were given lines. Because love of any sort is not taught through words, but by example. By bizarre and mysterious action, repetition, faith.

My mother loves me through worry, through horrible taste in bedding, through kicking my ass at Scrabble and never letting me win.

Be tough, my darling. The world has scared me. Don't get lost in the details. Stay warm. And strengthen your mind, which will be your saving grace.

My father loves me by letting me rest while watching football, by criticizing my taste in podcasts, by teaching me how to worry with intention and direction, usually about money or politics.

I see your mother's tendencies in you, so let's use them for the good of the world and not waste your time on frivolity. You're a child of God, and your work is important.

My lesson this Christmas is to be grateful for love in all forms. Worry. Faith. Courageous action.

Unexplained mystery.

What is yours?

SEVEN

Archetypes

I had an idea one day as I engaged with some friends embroiled in workplace drama. I lost track of the details of their work and the dynamics at play and heard stories I had heard a thousand times before from other people in different contexts.

These are characters, I thought. On the same day, I had a thoughtful conversation with another friend about personality tests that sort people into types and decided it would be a fun way to introduce people to the idea of boundaries. But each type was a character they had likely met before.

There is nothing magical about these archetypes. Some of them may feel familiar to you while others may seem works of fiction. They are based on my experiences in the world and the ways in which my behaviors have been echoed back to me. And yes, you read that right. I have engaged in behaviors that I identify with each of these types, so there is no shame. I encourage you to see which archetypes resonate with you and mirror your behavior and which relate to other people in your life. Then, look at how to make changes to your own behavior, or practice responses to the behavior of others, and change your life.

Type 1: The Chameleon

Mantra: Let's do whatever you want to do. Always.

Chameleon's boundaries let too much of the outside world in rather than defaulting to their own identity ("Oh, look, I can be green, too!"). They may not know themselves or may be afraid to show their true colors.

I often think of the stereotypes of teenage girls that influenced my upbringing—the teenage experience of the 1980s and 1990s. One would always conform to the needs of the group to try to fit in. More recently, I've noticed this in friends as they borrow the identity, interests, and desires of their current love interest. If their partner really likes football, they become an artificial enthusiast. If the next partner loves baking, they enroll in baking classes, deck out the kitchen, and abandon football. Each interest ebbs and flows with the partnership.

You might find yourself saying, "But wait, what about discovering new interests? What about compromise, getting outside of your comfort zone, and finding something you enjoy together?"

Those things are fantastic. Let's look at the nuance.

The chameleon takes another person's interests as

their own and then discards them along with the relationship. Think of the lizard walking from environment to environment—try on one outfit, then another, then change colors again. The problem with the human living the chameleon archetype is that it is exhausting. They are trying to make themselves into something they are not. Perhaps the chameleon meets someone who loves football and otherwise has no opinion about the sport.

They think, "I could like football, I've never tried!" They watch a few games, do a little research, buy a jersey.

They dislike it. It is not enjoyable or interesting. But they keep trying to convince themselves and throw themselves into it head-first. They start to feel resentful of how much of their time and life energy is consumed by football. After a while, they ask their partner to try something they enjoy, like yoga, and the partner doesn't like it. They don't even pretend to like it, and resentment accelerates until there is a confrontation or the relationship collapses.

"What do you mean you won't pretend to like yoga? I pretend to like football *all* the time for you, and *you don't even appreciate that I have given you all the Sundays of my life*," whimpers the chameleon.

"Wait…you don't like football?" the partner asks. "You've been lying to me?"

Yes, chameleon, you have. Pretending to like something you don't is lying. Even if you're doing it to be nice or to get along. In a relationship with healthy boundaries, it goes like this:

"I could like football, I've never tried!"

Try attending some games and then having a heart-to-heart with the partner.

"I enjoy spending time with you, but I don't enjoy football. I'm so happy for you to have your football needs met by other people. If there are important football events you'd like me to attend, I'm happy to come to two per year. I will be enthusiastic; I will wear the jersey and I will prepare a dip of seven layers. I will even paint my darn toenails the colors of the team, and I will love that I am supporting you."

And that's it. Honest, simple. While it might end the relationship, it's unlikely.

The rest of the Sundays, while the partner is footballing, the recovered chameleon is trying yoga, basket weaving, learning to shadowbox, or taking up archery. Or all of the above while they uncover the things that actually light them up.

The chameleon never gives their partner an opportunity to get to know the real them. They present an image of who they *think* their partner wants them to be—also a football enthusiast—instead of someone who is willing to very occasionally be a football enthusiast but would prefer to spend weekends climbing or weaving or figuring out what they love to do. This snowballs as the chameleon hops from relationship to relationship, constantly shapeshifting and running into the same cycles of negative behavior in each one because they have not been themselves.

How to Reclaim Your True Colors

If you find that you have adorable chameleon behaviors, read the *Who Am I Really* section and start to volunteer your opinion. You may notice that these behaviors pop up in other relationships as well at work, at home, in friendships, and in your faith tradition. If the office is trying to decide where to order lunch, make a suggestion. Practice voicing your true opinion (with kindness).

This isn't something that happened to me on a grand scale in romantic or friend relationships, but it did happen with food. My ex-husband had celiac disease, so his dietary restrictions had the last vote about the food that came into the house and where we went out to dine. I became accustomed to considering his needs first when we were eating together, but I would still eat gluten when I went out by myself or with friends. I did not bring it into the house because it would have made him sick. To me, this was a healthy compromise and not chameleon behavior.

However, in my next relationship, I was with a very controlling person who had strong opinions and judgements about what food I ate and brought into the house. While I had always enjoyed cooking and grocery shopping, I noticed that in that relationship, I did neither. When the relationship ended, I went to the grocery store for the first time in two years and was completely overwhelmed. I couldn't decide what to eat.

For a solid year, I ate kitchari, macaroni and cheese, eggs with broccoli, and oatmeal. After 18 months, I decided I needed to get over my fears and spend some quality time at Whole Foods. Every Friday night, I took myself on a date. I budgeted $100 and two hours and walked around the aisles looking for what sounded good to me. I cried the first eight times, as I could not understand how I had lost the ability to know what I wanted to eat. But eventually, with a lot of practice, I hit my stride. I didn't always like what I bought, but I started to remember what it was like to advocate and choose for myself.

It still hits me sometimes. When someone asks me to choose a restaurant, especially when it wasn't something I was anticipating, it stops me in my tracks. I have to really think about what I want to eat and not allow stories from the past or thoughts about what the other person might want to influence me. Sometimes I say "soup" or "quesadillas," and a lot of the time I say "macaroni and cheese." And these are not restaurants. But they give me somewhere to start.

What was once resignation about decision, deferment, or disengagement is now effort and full honesty. I don't always know what I want to eat. I haven't had a lot of practice at deciding. But now, I practice deciding, which means I have learned that I need to coach my co-diners on my process. I need a minute. I have to get quiet and see if there is any direction inside of my body about what I want to eat. Then I share what I know. Then, if it isn't helpful, I say "Chipotle."

Because everyone always wants Chipotle. I don't even know why this is a question.

(And yes, I'm serious).

Type 2: The Wanker

Mantra: "I can't hear you over my unsolicited advice and opinions."

Wankers have boundaries made of Swiss cheese, often letting too much out. They might over-share facts and unsolicited advice, but the biggest baddies are the unfiltered opinions. Self-awareness is fantastic, as is teaching and sharing perspective, but if you cannot seem to stop yourself from "saying it like it really is" and your name is not Dr. Phil…it's worth looking at this one.

I really wanted to name this one "the asshole," but I also needed to find it adorable.

Wanker behavior is an unskillful way of helping someone avoid a consequence of their behavior or of supporting someone in learning from your learning.

Wankers abound. The self-appointed captain of my former homeowners' association was notorious for telling everyone else exactly how to live their lives, from which pest control concoctions to spray on their potted plants to which BMW was the best. This person knew precisely which code in the bylaws any homeowner's unauthorized holiday decorations violated.

Unfortunately for all of us, wankers are not necessarily the people with adequate or even appropriate advice. Coaches and teachers often ask important questions or engage a level of curiosity, and other expert-level professionals like physicians and educators are plum tired of doling out advice. They fall into a unique category of anti-wankers, who probably *should* tell people about their questionable moles but don't.

I spent many years supporting new families through pregnancy and my first year postpartum. During that time, I learned that a number of common practices are actually quite dangerous. For example, it is dangerous to use a bucket car seat balanced on top of a grocery cart unless the cart is specifically designed for this. And it is inconvenient to put the car seat inside of the basket because it takes up most of the room and makes it harder to soothe the baby. So, people do the balancing act. Ninety-eight percent of the time, this is just fine. Very occasionally it can lead to a dangerous situation if the cart topples over, as it was not designed for this sort of load.

So, I would tell people.

At the grocery store.

Who I didn't know.

Who didn't ask me.

"Excuse me, do you know that what you're doing could potentially kill your child?"

(This is never received well).

Some people were polite, some were rude, and most were visibly irritated.

And this is the downside of wanker behavior—it's

quite isolating because it's often offensive. It's one of the many ways we distract ourselves from our own work: by focusing on the work of others. I don't have to sort out the pain of my divorce if I can direct my attention toward things that are none of my business.

When I do this, I'm often turning up the volume on an area of my life where I feel solid to distract you from the parts that feel unsteady. You will think I know everything and have it all figured out if I broadcast a loud message that I have it all together. Or I'll piss you off to the extent that you never get close enough to see or ask about my insecurities.

Avoiding being a wanker is simple but requires a little more self-awareness. Try asking people if they are open to your opinion or advice. Be prepared for them to say no. I sometimes physically clap my hand over my mouth as a reminder that no one was asking. The harder part is not taking that pent-up energy to the next encounter or complaining to a friend. Dump it into writing and then, if that doesn't give you some insight, connect with a friend and say, "I asked someone if they wanted my opinion and they didn't, and now I have feelings."

"Oh, good!" your friend can say. "Now you have some direction. What are the feelings? Who can you talk to about them to help you sort them out?"

It's that simple.

And never easy.

Type 3: The Victim

Mantra: "You'll never guess what happened to me now."

Victims wear their misfortunes like badges of honor. Uncomfortable, painful, and scary things happen in our lives. And people are legitimately victimized. This is distinct from playing the *role* of the victim.

It's really important that we understand the difference between being victimized and playing the role of the victim, because this can be a tender idea.

When you are victimized, you have no choices. If you are incarcerated, incapacitated, or restrained, you do not have choices. If you are a child, unable to advocate for yourself, or in an abusive relationship, you do not necessarily have choices. This is different from playing the role. The role of the victim is behaving as though you are incarcerated, incapacitated, or restrained when you are not (which is, hopefully, most of the time).

Here are some examples of victim statements:

"I can't get a divorce while my kids are still at home."

"I can't buy a house until my student loans are paid off."

"I could never wear that dress."

These are all choices shaded by victim goggles. I'm choosing not to get a divorce, not to buy a house, and not to wear that dress. It is incredibly difficult to snuff out all of the ways in which we do this because we would prefer not to own the responsibility for our circumstances. However, owning responsibility for our circumstances gives us direction and power to do something differently.

Imagine the reality of the divorce. Many people believe that they can't get a divorce while their kids are still at home. But, at least in the United States at the time of this writing, it is legal to get divorced with children. I'm sure there is science on all sides of the issue, but the notion that children raised by two married parents who despise one another are happier, better-adjusted, and will thrive better as adults is silly. There are plenty of well-adjusted, productive, and pleasant adults whose parents were married, divorced, or never met. It's even possible for parents to demonstrate a healthy relationship as they evolve from marriage into divorce.

If the kids are 17.5 years old, the paperwork is monstrous, and it makes rational sense to wait, the statement is still, "I'm choosing not to get divorced while my kids are at home."

If you believe you cannot buy a home until all your student loans are paid off, then I'd like you to make friends with a realtor. Ask how many of their clients are completely debt-free prior to purchasing homes. Maybe your priority is paying off or paying down your student loans prior to taking on another huge helping of debt, but again, the priority is a choice. If you don't qualify for a loan because your debt-to-income ratio is out of whack, that's another challenge, but it still doesn't make the statement above true. You might need to prioritize getting a better job, marrying a Sultan, or looking outside of the greater Los Angeles area for a home. Real estate is cheaper in many parts of the country. Owning is not for everyone. Get clear on the numbers and clear on the truth. "I'm choosing not to buy a home until I pay down x amount of my student loans."

You can wear that dress—trust me. The only reason you can't is you think you can't. You can order or make it in your size or have it tailored. You don't have to wear it to the country club, but you can wear it. A dress does not have power over you. No matter your size, gender, age, or level of fitness, you outrank the dress.

Wear it.

(Get your tissues.)

For many years, I struggled with infertility, which is perhaps the understatement of my life. I was destroyed by the experience of my own body betraying me. While I wasn't held captive, I sure thought I was. Every time someone told me they were pregnant, it felt like a personal attack. What was worse was that I owned a prenatal yoga studio and worked as a doula and midwife's assistant. My life was built around pregnancy and birth, so all my friends were in the realm of birth.

Great story, right?

Irony, drama, etc.

The big, dark secret about my infertility was that I chose not to pursue medical means of getting pregnant. It was and remains my choice that I want my body to be healthy enough to get pregnant. I'm unwilling to take Western medicines and hormone injections to force my body to be pregnant.

That's a choice.

I also did not believe I was in a place where I could consider adoption. Conversations with my husband continued to reaffirm that he was not as interested or invested in parenthood as I was, and I blamed him for closing that door.

But it wasn't closed. I could have pursued adoption and I didn't. And I still can.

Today, instead of saying, "Guess I'll never be a mom," I get to step out of the role of the victim and identify the truth, which is that I'm unwilling to take the physical actions necessary to force my body to get pregnant, and I'm not yet ready to step into the world of adoption.

I have choices.

It is painful to take ownership of our condition, which is why we play the victim role. However, it's a manipulative way of getting what we want—trading our story for compassion, empathy, pity, and attention. We know what we need, but our way of getting it is...icky. When we have a sense of control, we can ask for specific help in finding the resources we need.

The remedy to the victim trap is to remember you have a choice. Even if the choices are ridiculous, illegal, or less savory than the ones we're choosing, we remember we have a choice. And poof! The spell is broken.

Type 4: The Rescuer

Mantra: "I've never met a person—er, problem—I couldn't fix."

Rescuers find purpose, meaning, and distraction from their own suffering by helping others. Generosity is incredible, but rescuing is often a down payment on future expectations. Our culture teaches us there is something noble about swooping in and saving someone from the consequences of their actions. We love and idealize the rescuer. I've come to question this because "saving someone from the consequences of their actions" happens to be my definition of codependency.

A key difference between generosity and rescuing is the ego's involvement. If you can contribute an action or send money anonymously, you're in the clear. Your ego is not involved. If it is important for the recipient of your generous action to know that you were the actor or the giver, then this is 100 percent ego. You're hoping to get something in return.

Is that so bad?

I don't know...are you ever disappointed?

The rescuer and the victim are roles we play, and they are not the healthiest roles. The victim allows themselves to be abused to have a story to tell, and the rescuer exchanges money, time, or energy for a sense of pride and self-respect. Rescuers form the second point in the victim triangle.

Rescuers require victims to exist. In the triangle, the rescuer saves the victim from the abuser. In fiction you often see these three roles as separate and different characters, but in reality, one individual can pass between all these roles like a game of hot potato. It's great drama from the outside but really wretched and exhausting on the inside.

Rescuing is saving someone from their circumstances, which is different from helping, supporting, or resourcing. It is so ingrained in the fabric of our culture that we often can't help falling in love with our rescuers (unless we have been abused by a rescuer before). Rescuing should be reserved for life and death circumstances—lifeguards, firefighters, medical professionals, and the occasional good Samaritan with a strong truck and a tow strap. These folks are usually compensated—it is generally their occupation to provide this skill.

Helping is excellent. When you are unable to do something, you need help. You need to identify that you need help and ask for it. It's even better if you know what help you need. Even if you don't, simply saying out loud that you need help is an excellent step.

The hard part for someone playing the role of the rescuer is to hear the request and let it go—or refer it to someone else. Even if it is something you can do, check your motives. If your motivation is to win attention or affection, or to avoid feeling the discomfort of your own circumstances, then pass it along or contact someone on your higher council, stat.

This gets complicated in relationships where the parent/child power dynamic is at work. The parent often has resources the child does not, and the child must ask permission or advocate for their needs. In learning how to do this, some find the victim role to be a really effective way of getting what they want. The parent can also find significant satisfaction from playing the rescuer role. Some of us carry these parent/child relationships into our friendships and intimate partnerships and continue playing out the dysfunction.

A seemingly innocuous example from my life: I had a friend preparing to travel internationally to do service work and he had low cash flow. I knew he was going somewhere food would be plentiful but that he might not meet all of his dietary needs. He got sick several times on his previous trip, so I gifted him $100 to buy vitamins and medications, even though he didn't ask. Instead of vitamins, he bought a guitar case so he could bring his guitar on the trip.

I had feelings about this. (Mostly resentment.)

I was frustrated that he didn't buy vitamins even though I hadn't shared the intention behind my gift or asked if it would be helpful; it was a nice reminder that I was engaging in rescuing behavior, because it was a down payment on a future expectation. I thought I was buying a specific outcome; when I didn't get it, I was disappointed.

Why do I care?

Well, solving his problems (even if they were imaginary problems I projected onto him) was easier than dealing with my own feelings in that moment. It felt like an expression of love and care. But, in reality, the health and well-being of a friend is not my responsibility. I can express love and care by saying I want him to be healthy and happy. Perhaps bringing a guitar with him will contribute to his wellbeing, and who am I to judge what's best for him? Am I his parent? No. I'm his friend, which also means that if he calls me in three months with a nutritional deficiency, I can know that it is entirely his responsibility. And I don't have to listen to him complain.

The other big reason we rescue is to avoid seeing someone have a feeling or experience disappointment. Unfortunately, this is also ego. If you help because it hurts to see someone hurt, that is human. If you rescue someone from their feeling as a way to rescue yourself from feeling, that's avoidance.

For example, if your spouse forgets their lunch at home, you might take it to them. That would be really kind and likely unnecessary, but is it rescuing?

If you are doing it to be perceived as the rescuer.

If you are doing it in lieu of your own responsibilities.

If you are doing it because them not having their packed lunch makes you feel sad.

Ask yourself if it is easy, if it doesn't require you to rearrange your life, and if it brings you joy. If so, go for it! If you feel resentment as you do it, fear as you contemplate it, or a rapid pulse for any reason, talk to someone about it and get to the bottom of your motivation. It is so subtle, and really, you don't have to decide on your own. This is an area where it helps to consult your HC.

Type 5: The Abuser

Mantra: I'm a nice person as long as no one else is around.

First of all, if you are in a relationship where you are being abused, you must leave. ***You must end the relationship, and you must find support to do this that is not a self-improvement book.***

Or any book.

There is a difference between playing the role of the abuser and being an abusive person. Rarely will someone step forward and identify as playing the role of the abuser. Just know if you are playing the victim or the rescuer, you are also well-prepared to play the abuser. Abusers are low-functioning victims—they perceive themselves to be trapped and do not have the skills to say so or ask for appropriate help. They are rabid dogs. Their distress comes out sideways and they strike at anything and everything, especially people who stay close and try to pet them.

Do not engage. Create space. Call for help.

In that order.

My brother asked me what I wanted for Christmas and I sent him a picture of a particular travel mug. On Christmas morning, I unwrapped something that was decidedly different. The expression on my face told my mother that it wasn't what I asked for.

Apparently, my brother didn't have time to go shopping, so he tried to convey my request to my mother (victim). She went out and bought something (rescuer) and it wasn't right (guess who I am?).

Without me saying a word, my mother said we could go to REI and exchange it, no problem. I explained why I wanted the other mug and said I would love the opportunity to exchange it. When we got to REI, we found something similar to what I wanted, and I was happy with it. My mother insisted we go out to the car to confirm it fit in my cup holder before purchasing it. I assured her it would fit and that even if it didn't, I would still prefer it over the other mug. She was insistent. She did not want to do this exchange again.

I yelled. At my mother. In REI. As a 38-year-old woman, I had a tantrum. I became the abuser.

Then I felt bad about it for the next six hours, cried in the car as I drove the two hours home, and eventually called her and apologized. This is how I can confirm I was the abuser—the remorse and self-loathing.

Abusers are trapped victims. I was having an internal pity party regarding a terrible experience in the previous days that I didn't want to talk about. I was pretending everything in my life was "just fine," so the holiday family dynamics laid the perfect groundwork for me to explode.

I do not have an abusive relationship with my mother. I did not belittle, gaslight, or otherwise emotionally abuse her. If you're unclear, it's important to get very, very clear about whether you're dealing with a toad or with poison.

Toxic Relationships

You may find yourself in a place with digestive distress, fatigue, anxiety, and overwhelm and not rightly know that it is in large part due to a toxic relationship in your life.

The business world tells us to make lists of pros and cons, and we inappropriately apply this concept to interpersonal relationships. It makes sense in business. Should we buy this property? Pros. Cons. Simple —okay, not really, but simpler than what I'm about to show you.

When we look at a toxic relationship, we often rationalize the reasons we must stay by listing the assets. What are the "pros" of this person? Perhaps they are wealthy, attractive, kind, effusive with praise, generous, intelligent, compassionate, and grateful. In the case of every abusive relationship I've encountered, they are on the A+ side of most of these qualities. Incredible qualities that you would be a fool to cut out of your life. I will use the metaphor of making a smoothie here—these are the blueberries, the spinach, the almond milk, and the protein powder.

Everyone has bad days, grumpy moods, sadness, anger, and their own host of adorable neuroses and pet peeves. Everyone is entitled to be a toad—to yell, to storm off into isolation, to donate all of their clothes on a whim, or to dry the sink after washing the dishes. These are cons or, per Dan Savage, "the price of admission." They are part of the story of the person, and it isn't your job to fix or change them.

Your job is to embrace them for all of their qualities and permit them adequate time and space to toad. In the smoothie analogy, these might be the bitter greens or a scoop of ice cream—if you're aiming for healthy and delicious these complicate things, but they aren't a deal breaker.

But.

This is not to be confused with deplorable behavior. Deplorable behavior is abuse, which I can spell out for you. Physical violence is easier to see, but emotional terrorism, manipulation, and gaslighting are also intolerable, inexcusable, and comparable to cyanide in your smoothie. It does not matter how good the goodness is (and it may top out the most incredible of the goodness scale), cyanide is poison and the smoothie will kill you.

Dealing with an abusive person is like fighting a forest fire or wrangling a dangerous, rabid wild animal.

It's better not to.

While you're working to get out of an abusive situation, the following strategies may be helpful, depending on your circumstances:

Be at your best. Well-rested, fully nourished, and healthy. If you aren't all three of these things, you're too vulnerable.

Protect yourself. Know when you need to get out. What are the signs that you must leave? Create a specific list of deal breaker behaviors that are grounds for ending the conversation. It is appropriate to share these with the other person.

Have adequate protection. In this case, acknowledgement and "back pocket" phrases like "I heard you" or "thank you for telling me" or "I'm not sure how to respond right now" are helpful when you are prone to reaction. Have professionals on hand for strategy and debrief.

Understand your limitations. You did not cause the animal to be wild. Nothing you do will fix or "un-wild" the animal. You are engaging for a specific purpose, and it cannot be to fix the animal.

You will not be able to do this forever. It takes a lot out of you. At some point, this relationship must end, and you must define when that is for yourself. Create a timeline or list of specific deal breaker behaviors that are grounds for ending the relationship.

Stick to them, no question.

If you feel queasy, uneasy, or possibly like you might have an extremely urgent bowel movement, please call a trusted friend right this very minute. Abusive relationships end in death, and if your body is telling you that you are in mortal danger, you must now ask for help and make a plan with a team.

Archetype 6: The Decathlete

Mantra: "I'm too busy being too busy...and yes, I can have your homework done by five."

If you live and work in the world, you are likely to have periods of overwhelm in your life, especially if you are driven, an entrepreneur, or a parent. Perpetual overwhelm is an indication that your boundaries could use some work. FOMO is real, and there is tremendous value in being productive and sharing your gifts.

This is you if:

You only rest when you are physically so sick that you literally cannot get out of bed.

You have considered brushing your teeth while eating a sandwich. In the shower. To save time.

You have not said no in, well…ever.

Overwhelm is a choice or pattern decathletes use to distract themselves from their own experience. Of all of the types I have created here, this is the one I relate with most. I like to feel productive because I forget that I am a worthy, worthwhile person whether or not I accomplish anything. I can make a vacation "work" by having a list and a plan.

Can you relate?

You may be this person, or you may have someone in your life who is this person. It's difficult to embrace that we cause and foster the chaos in our own lives, but decathletes do this like it is an Olympic sport. Work! Volunteering! Obligations! Javelin!

Just like all archetypes, this cluster of adorable behaviors tells us we are uncomfortable and trying to control or manipulate. Instead of illegal drugs, alcohol, sex, video games, or social media, we work as though the work will never end, or we parent as though our child is incapable of learning or functioning on their own.

In Colorado, which is where I have almost always lived (I tried California for the first year of my adulthood and it's lovely, but you can have it), people work hard and play hard. They are up early running, yoga-ing and CrossFit-ing, then they're off to the office job or computer. Here they require multiple technological devices to stay connected to all of the internets at once and do not break for lunch. Then they do happy hour work, return home to work, and pass out.

Oh, they do this where you live too?

I made yoga my part-time and then full-time career, so even my "pre-work" or "post-work" fitness was also work. Here is a list of jobs I've had since graduating from college with a fancy degree:

- Health center assistant
- Regional director of education for a major nonprofit
- Interim director of an assisted living facility
- Regional fundraising director for a major nonprofit
- Board member for job placement nonprofit
- Camp Jeep counselor
- Stage manager for several local theatre companies
- Client care coordinator for a regional nonprofit
- Assistant director of admissions
- Interpersonal dynamics consultant
- Lead trainer for a yoga teacher training
- Associate lead for many, many yoga teacher trainings

- Co-owner of a yoga studio
- Doula
- Midwife's assistant
- Owner of my own consulting company
- Web developer
- Database consultant
- Recruiting consultant
- Director of retreats for an international yoga company
- Freelance writer
- Ghost writer
- Nanny
- Babysitter

In the span of 15 years, I've somehow made work my life's work. My color-coded calendar lets me know who I'm working for (as in who to bill) for each engagement, and while purple is on the calendar, it did not have a place of prominence until the end of 2016 when I hit rock bottom and decided to do everything differently. Until then, and to this day, you'll see that my lists have lists. I have almost everything partially done and will accomplish almost everything on time without you knowing that it is causing me emotional distress. If I look back before the time where I was eligible to work, I would do the same thing while baking. I would bake six different things simultaneously, just to see if I could do it. Juggle baking. For no reason other than I needed a distraction from coping.

I love lists, crossing things off of them, and

keeping track of things. Having a lot to do and getting it done gives me a false sense that I'm in control. The same is true with contingency plans. When one area of my life is out of my control, such as when I'm waiting for the doctor to call with test results, I try to maximize my efficiency and effectiveness by juggling as many things as possible at once.

> **Aside**: *There are circumstances that incite overwhelm that are not self-imposed. Poverty, new parenthood, and caring for an ill family member may make you feel like a decathlete, but are not an indication of shitty boundaries.*

Decathletes might also have a problem or two with money. This could be a manifestation of how they "force" themselves into saying yes all the time. I did this.

While my parents did an excellent job of telling me how to *save* money, nowhere did I discover how much money it might be reasonable to *earn*. So much of my work was done as a volunteer, on a paltry stipend, or at $10 per hour. Decathletes are often compulsive under-earners, which legitimizes their over-work. If you find yourself relating to the decathlete, do not despair. Instead, leverage your higher council to determine the adorable ways that you are keeping yourself in your adorable patterns. Enlist the support of a therapist (or two) who are there to support you when your coping mechanism disappears.

Other decathletes are affectionately known as "helicopter parents." These are the folks who spend their time cutting sandwiches into shapes, advocating for extra credit, or nosing into their children's social lives to bypass their own experience.

There is absolutely nothing wrong with cutting sandwiches into shapes. If you are a sandwich artist and it brings you joy, it is absolutely your art and I am enthusiastic in your continued expression. If, however, you find yourself busying yourself with sandwich art which your ungrateful children never appreciate, or you are doing it in order to impress other parents via your excessive posting, I am here to tell you this is not great parenting. It's not relevant to parenting. At all. You get zero good parenting points for sandwich shapes—if you're doing it for points.

When I worked in the world of college admission, I encountered parents who had 18+ years' experience hovering and meddling. These parents experienced a high degree of distress upon sending their kids off to a residential college in another state. A small handful would call me, the admission rep, on the regular to check in on their student. Even going as far as suggesting I maybe take them out for lunch and see how they were adapting. (This is spying.)

I politely declined and suggested they redirect their highly attuned hypervigilance toward under-resourced high school and college-aged folks nearer their home—like international students or those from financially weak origins, rather than paying a married 30-something to spy on and/or date their 18-year-old.

Adorable tendencies are often talents gone sideways or behaviors that can be honed into talents.

Except for decathletes. Overwork will always be there. Overparenting will always be a possibility, and this will be rewarded either financially or with loads of kudos.

The caring side is there. Some people have more love in their hearts than people in their lives. If that is the case, feeding someone who needs food or listening to someone who has no one is medicine for both. Dig into the need and separate it from the intended target.

Unless the need is busy, in which case the remedy is to hold still and phone a therapist.

Archetype 7: The Royal

Mantra: "Alexa—park my car."

Are you completely incapable of caring for yourself? (Ok, this is a trick question.)

Everyone is incapable of caring for themselves *completely*—we are interdependent beings. But if you are unable to meet your basic needs (and it's not because you're ill or injured; it's simply a pattern that has developed in your life), you might benefit from looking at your boundaries. Where the decathlete finds meaning and purpose from saying yes and juggling everyone else's needs to stay busy, the royal finds meaning and connection by needing things. I think of the nineteenth century Southern belle whose entire life purpose was to be cared for by others. We all need connection, and it's not reasonable to assume that we will be proficient at absolutely everything we need or want. But the royal has pushed way, way beyond healthy interdependence into constant dependence.

I see this often with parents and their adult children. It goes both ways. The parent might call the child to come do some work on a ladder, as it is no longer safe for them—and how excellent to identify a need (ladder work) that is outside the scope of your reasonable capacity (falling is actually quite a big deal) and request appropriate help! But equally good is hiring a professional.

Likewise, an adult child might come over to do laundry at their parents' house because their other laundry option is the laundromat, because their laundry facilities are on the fritz, or because they are exchanging ladder work for laundry service. It's possible that it's more enjoyable for everyone to enjoy a meal or a chat at home while the machines do their magic—but also, when or if it's possible, equally good is hiring a laundry service.

Neither ladders nor laundry on their own are inappropriate, but if these favors and services are always one-sided and without any sense of reciprocity, there might be a problem. Parents sometimes believe that their adult children "owe them" for all of the time, energy, and effort they spent rearing them. This dysfunctional belief can facilitate entitled royal behavior. "I raised and fed you for 18 years, the least you could do is come over and change my light bulbs."

My opinion about this is that you are responsible for the health and survival of your children until they are 18.

That's the jam, and that's the end. It cannot be a down payment on how you will be treated beyond that time. If, however, you pay for them to go to medical school, you could reasonably say, "I will pay for your medical school, but you'd better believe that if I have a medical question, I expect you to answer it. *For the rest of my life.*"

Reciprocity, see?

The adult child can sometimes leverage their child-like, royal behavior because they do not have the skills to transition to adult-adult relationships with their parents. They might come over and do their laundry well into their 30s, or leverage some perceived helplessness to unskillfully maintain their sense of intimacy with their parents. If they are not capable of doing their own laundry, they can learn or hire a service. The need is always there; the dependency need not be.

People in any relationship can leverage royal tendencies—it's called entitlement. Expecting favors from a colleague, boss, or friend is problematic. Instead, ask for a favor and call a spade a spade. I know I'm asking for a favor, for something extra—you get to say no or counteroffer with whatever feels appropriate. Royal behavior is always enabled by reciprocal over-giving and over-caring behavior.

A workplace example: employee A is a whiz at spreadsheets. They can make a pivot table in seconds, locate the source of rogue errors, and quickly create charts and graphs that are both beautiful and easy to understand. Employee B employs false helplessness: "I don't know *anything* about spreadsheets. Employee A, can you do mine?"

The appropriate answers?

"Yes, for a price," and "No."

I actually do not believe that you need to be good or even proficient at everything. You are (probably) not Martha Stewart or Bob Villa, and neither of them is good at absolutely everything either. In fact, I believe it is totally appropriate for work to be assigned based on training, talents, and experience. If you've got a spreadsheet whiz on your team, please invite them to do the bulk of the spreadsheeting. In a workplace where the management gets this idea, Employees A and B can come to an agreement to reassign their own tasks. The appropriate "price" for having A do the spreadsheet magic might be B taking a few calls for A, doing a bit of graphic design, or reordering their business cards. It doesn't need to be a dollar value exchange, but it must steer clear of entitlement and resentment.

Type 8: The Pirate

Mantra: "What rules?"

Are you a lone wolf?

Are you (honestly) more interested in what you want than what is right?

Does the word "compromise" end conversations with you?

Pirates do not care what anyone else thinks, wants, or needs. And while a healthy sense of your own desires is valuable, prioritizing them at the expense of those who depend (and interdepend) on you is a recipe for disaster. No one is a pirate all of the time—not even your weird uncle—but the pirate is a role we play when we are not at our best.

Pirates often end friendships over losing an argument, change their identities to win (at any cost), and stuff their feelings down, down, way down, practicing emotional mutiny. Akin to abusers, pirates broadcast their needs with words or actions and do not have the bandwidth to consider anything other than their most fundamental perspective.

All of us are capable of lying, cheating, and stealing, and we all have. Maybe you haven't joined a band of hooligans to overtake a neighboring vessel, but you have had very low-functioning moments. You have sunk to a level that you'd be happy not to have broadcast on social media.

Road rage, anyone?

I am that woman who drives to yoga in a full-blown rage. Worse, I'm often the teacher. Even worse? I'm often there to teach yoga teachers. On my way, I am screaming, driving erratically, and employing the language of a sailor.

"Who am I?" I ask myself. This is not an everyday experience. My rage is episodic, and usually misdirected, as I find myself irrationally homicidal about someone trying to turn left.

"Why is *everyone* turning *left* today?"

Which is the wrong question. My adorable pirate tendencies give me the opportunity to ask the right question, which is, "Why is it so irritating to me today that people are turning left?"

Because I am in a hurry. I left home too late, and I think that being late means I am worthless. Because I am afraid I am missing out on something. As I narrow in, I know I need to call someone and chat it out. "Knowing what you know about me, can you figure out why I just screamed myself red in the face at a group of schoolchildren crossing the street when they had the right of way?"

Also?

Binging on anything—sugar, social media, porn, or shopping—is a big ol' flag that you're on the high seas aboard the wrong ship. You are not entitled to another glass of red wine, all the cookies in the box, or an evening with the internet. The same way you are not entitled to someone else's wallet or car, especially if this thing is a secret. (*Binging is stealing from yourself, my darling.*)

You get to eat, drink, and watch anything you want. You really do. I'm not telling you that you should feel shame for anything in particular. I'm suggesting that if you do feel shame about anything, want to keep it secret, and need a complicated treasure map to locate it (or hide it from yourself), you have a beautiful opportunity. You can chat about it with a thoughtful group of people who do the same sort of thing. Ask other people anything.

You don't have to agree with other people; just remember they exist and that their opinions are also valid. If you want your way all the time, every time, you'll be swashbuckling solo for the long haul.

Type 9: The Astronaut

Mantra: "I'll just hold my breath and see what happens..."

Astronauts are on an extended, solitary vacation from relationships, preferring space and tending towards isolation. This is not the same thing as being an introvert or being fueled by time alone in private reflection. Solitude is medicine, and most of us don't get enough of it. But isolation is poison, as we know from every neighbor of every serial killer ever interviewed.

"[Person in question] was always quiet, polite and kept to themselves."

I'm not saying isolation will make you a serial killer, but it's unlikely to support you in enjoying your life and being a thriving, productive member of society.

Everyone needs personal space, but if you're taking it because you believe your needs are harmful to others, you might benefit from looking at that belief.

This has been me.

Maybe there were some moments in my childhood when I felt like I was a burden to my parents and caregivers (because I'm sure I was), but it really wasn't until much later in my life that I noticed my adorable internal monologue externalized at a romantic partner.

"I'm sorry for *existing*."

This is different from suicidal ideation. It might be more insidious, because we don't recognize the slippery slope of gently withdrawing into ourselves one need at a time, silencing requests one by one, or withholding our entirely valid and relevant opinions.

See how easy I am to get along with? I have no needs. Yup. I'm just fully self-sufficient and don't need your attention, affection, or reassurance. Just floating in outer space. Holding my breath. Hoping someone will notice without me having to advocate for myself...

If your boundaries are made of concrete and barbed wire and you are unwilling to actively express your wants and needs, they will come out sideways. You will attempt to meet them by talking to your dolls or cats or the cast of your favorite TV show.

The way out (or back in?) is to practice making a tiny connection. Ask for help from a store employee. Strike up a conversation with someone at a coffee shop. Send a message in a bottle to a safe person. Carve out a tiny piece of the world where you feel safe to express a need, even if it is very small and simple.

Having needs means being honest.

Type 10: The Martyr

Mantra: "Am I the only one working around here?"

Do you feel like you're underwater trying to keep someone else's head above? Like, the whole family, department, company, or country? Are you single-handedly responsible for life on Earth? Do you feel like you are sometimes?

Martyrs love to feel needed or pitied. It's a truly crummy way of determining their worth. Similar to the decathlete, the martyr is way overworked and likely underpaid (otherwise they're just a rich jerk and sort of a pathetic martyr).

I noticed this in myself once at a yoga studio. I was there to teach the yoga classes (a very important thing). However, I often found I was also there to change the paper towels in the restroom, as it seemed no one else in the facility was capable of doing so. They were large, industrial roles that fit into those stupid locked dispensers, so clients actually could not replace them themselves without the key thing. It's important to change the paper, but doing so did not make me feel important. It felt beneath me. It felt like I was the only one paying attention, the only one putting in the extra effort, "...*the only one working around here!*"

Maybe you are the only one who cleans the community microwave at work, or puts gas in the car, or even notices "*the filth!*" You don't have to be. It's possible you have different standards of what it means to be "out" of toothpaste or different ideas of what the acceptable level of cleanliness is for a food container. But sometimes it's even simpler than that. No one else notices because you just do it. *Ugh.*

This was the case with the paper towels. No one else was annoyed by it, because they understood it was not their job and because eventually someone did it. I was the one seething under a mountain of resentment, shooting daggers at the teachers. Because I was an even *more* important teacher of teachers (or maybe because one day I was reading about selfless service), I had an epiphany. I decided to reorient the team regarding their responsibilities. Each teacher training became an opportunity to invite and empower the folks to change out the paper towels themselves (which was actually pretty tricky). My resentment vanished, the studio was almost always well-stocked, and I returned to taking a turn in the paper towel duty rotation.

You won't get your way all the time, but you also don't have to suffer all the time. Healthy boundaries include knowing what you're willing to offer and what you need to receive in exchange. Resentment is your red flag, as is bragging about your "selfless service." Because if it's selfless, you don't need to brag about it, right?

This is you if:

- You find yourself always "taking one for the team."
- You believe that everything is fine, as long as you are the only one getting hurt.
- You continue going when everyone else has asked you to stop.

One way to keep people from walking over you is not lying down in the middle of the floor. You get to have specific non-negotiables in your life, so pick them and stick to them.

Type 11: The Magician

Mantra: "Nothing but pent-up emotions up my sleeve."

Do you hide behind the illusion that everything is fine?

In 12-step rooms, "fine" is an acronym for "frustrated, insecure, neurotic, and emotional." I would argue I've never heard someone describe their emotional state as fine and actually mean equanimous, which is what it is supposed to mean. Whenever I think of "fine," I think of the stereotypical parent yelling at their child to clean up their room, then turning to answer the phone with a very pleasant tone of voice.

I have this relationship with my dog, who sees the absolute worst in me and is simultaneously the only living being permitted to shit on my bathroom floor. I try to sing at her rather than yelling, but when she steps on my face in the night, I have been known to wake the dead. Magician behaviors are lopsided because there is no confidant and no outlet. Magicians simply stuff it all up their sleeves while dazzling us with a display of incredible wonder and togetherness. This is the stereotypical soccer mom, the Stepford wife, and occasionally a man like George Jetson (or any other paternal figure depicted on 1950s television).

In my case, once upon a lifetime ago, I was up for

a mega promotion. I did a marathon day of inter-viewing with everyone on staff, including doing a mock sales presentation for a few hundred of my closest colleagues, after which I was not awarded the position. So, unlike a normal failed job interview where you just go on to the next thing, I was the laughingstock of the entire company (in my own head).

I was massively pissed off for the rest of my tenure. It just so happens that not winning the job corresponded with a miscarriage, which I never told any of my colleagues about. Rather than confessing what was really bothering me, I showed everyone my misdirected rage at losing the job opportunity and kept my personal failings to myself.

Magicians value the way life looks at the expense of how it feels. They might treat friends and acquain-tances as lovely assistants to chop in half. Rather than true intimacy and friendship, they arrange the right people in the right places. If you recognize some magician tendencies in yourself, do not despair. Tell the truth in small doses to people with little influence on your life. Just say you're tired if you're tired.

Type 12: The Giver

Mantra: "You can't take it from me if I give it to you first!"

Would you give someone the shirt off of your back? That's not a bad thing—sometimes you have two shirts and they have none. Sometimes you're a paramedic, they're bleeding, and you need something to use as a tourniquet. I'm sure there are other good reasons to give someone the shirt you are wearing. What's more interesting to me is that this is a phrase used to describe someone who is selfless, which we think is a good thing.

Is it so good to be selfless?

It depends (of course) on your motivation.

I firmly believe you can only give from your excess, so if it is a two-shirt scenario, I think it's great. We have widely varied definitions of "excess," which are easiest to see in how we handle our finances. Some people start to tighten discretionary spending when they have $5,000 left in the bank. Others only cease when all their credit cards are maxed out and they get declined by a vendor. It's important for each of us to decide how we define it

Giving and *rescuing* can look the same, so I'll dig into the more nefarious side of giving.

The adorable archetype of giving is giving something you don't want to give because you don't want it to be taken.

Self-deprecating humor is a good example. Why on Earth would people make fun of themselves to make others laugh?

To keep the power.

I know I have freckles. If I felt insecure about it (as I did for the majority of my life), I might make jokes about it so no one else did, or so if they did, I wouldn't get hurt because I started it.

People may also do this with belongings, such as, "Oh this sweater would look much better on you anyway." But I see it more often with relational power dynamics. Like sex.

I have no idea how many women have told me they had sex with a man when they didn't want to because they thought they should. Or they did because they were afraid that if they didn't, he would end the relationship. Or they did because they wanted to retain the power and not be the one to say no. *I will have sex with you because I don't want to have to say no.* This may happen in relationships between people of all genders as a function of power, but my experience is limited to women.

Whether it's self-deprecating humor or having sex when you'd rather not, the adorable giving takes more from you than you have to give.

Givers often see others as more deserving than themselves. Generosity is wonderful, but it generally refers to reallocating excess without expectations. Like astronauts, givers dial down their own needs and desires to accommodate those of others.

This is you if:

- You ignore your own suffering.
- You get upset when someone uses a gift in a way you did not intend.
- You believe it is better, much better, to give than to receive.
- You feel the need to "settle up" if someone gives you time, energy, or a gift you do not believe you have earned.
- You would never, ever ask for help.

The next time you consider giving something, note your motivations. Are you doing what is culturally normal, like giving up your seat to an elderly person on a bus? Are you hoping to receive praise, recognition, or some other form of reciprocity? Would you feel the same way if your gift were received anonymously? Consider waiting and consulting a higher council to examine your motives before giving.

Interlude: Instruction Manuals

I'm vacuuming today.

Yesterday, my friend and her toddler came over to help me install a ceiling fan because earlier this week, the fan above my head decided the globe was ripe and dropped it right on me as I slept.

Knowing my limitations regarding electrical work and my lack of necessary limbs to both lift and unscrew simultaneously, I called in backup. Two tiny women in their thirties and a toddler.

(God help us.)

We watched a YouTube instructional video, which was a bit disconcerting. Nearly a quarter-million people have viewed it but it does not give success rates, nor are there any helpful Yelp reviews. The man started with "I had my home wired specifically..." and then I glazed over.

What?

We tried. We successfully removed parts A-T from the box, found the instruction manual, and were flummoxed by step one, which referred to an essential part that was not included. Fastid-

ious women that we are, we dutifully unpacked, unwound, counted, and inventoried, naming each part as we went. I secretly missed the useless yet comforting image of the man with the pencil behind his ear à la Ikea manuals.

Step one—find a man with a pencil.

(I'm pretty good at that step one.)

Without the easy first step, and without the essential part that was excluded from my purchase, we gave up, packing up most of the parts back in the box and shoving them underneath the guest bed.

This is what I do when an unmanageable problem surfaces in my life—first, call in backup. Second, give it the "college try." Third, shove it under something and pave over the emotions of failure with cheese, chocolate, or conversation. Wait for rain, the cavalry, or the apocalypse—whichever comes first.

The fan was a bust, but the day wasn't. Because instead of spending a few hours with a very confusing instruction manual and 20 different parts to assemble (some of which were not included, a conversation I intend to have with Mr. Lowe himself), we sat on the couch and watched the full joy of the experience of destroying Styrofoam packaging through the eyes of a child.

And today, I got to vacuum all of the tiny wispy bits of Styrofoam that remained. The static cling of them ensured I put in due effort, and I was grateful. As has been taught to me, be grateful for the dishes you must wash, as it means you have both dishes and meals. Be grateful for the laundry you need to fold, as it means you have plenty to wear.

Be grateful for the flotsam left in the wake of a joyful toddler, as it means your life has been touched by friends and by

God—her infinite wisdom that the joy of the thing was not the point of the thing.

That the fan will wait for another day, but that this moment is precious and sacred and would otherwise have been missed if we always kept things tidy and followed The Rules.

I am grateful for the wisdom of the child who shepherded my sanity on this day.

Who kept me walking in the light.

EIGHT

Ghosts and Monsters

Ever notice that sometimes you react to an abrasive text message in a calm, collected fashion and sometimes you launch into a vengeful rage?

I call this the text monster, and it exists in all of us.

The text monster reacts rather than responding. The text monster adds nuance and intonation where it may not have been intended and jumps into worst-case-scenario mode. The text monster is always present and will sabotage your friendships and relationships if given access to your phone.

Reacting and responding are different. I'm not the first person to distinguish the two, but for the sake of this section I'll define reacting as the text monster. Texting is a great place to examine this behavior. We often perceive urgency with texts—it's not a call, where we have vocal nuances, nor is it an email, where we have a moment of reflection before hitting send. It is a text message—an instant telegram we can fire back at without a second thought.

Or a first thought.

Many of us employ this reactive *burn it down* mentality to ending relationships—whether it's after a pinnacle fight, storming out of an office building never to return, or posting something inciteful, dangerous, or toxic on social media. Burning bridges is a really effective way of ensuring that the other party keeps their distance—you've acted in such an immature or frightening way that they would never consider repairing the relationship.

Responding is so different from reacting. It is consideration and reflection, thoughtful and complete. Frankly, we rarely make the time for this. If we don't burn down a relationship with a person or an entity, we often go to the other end of the spectrum: ghosting.

Ghosting

I did not fully appreciate the commonplace nature of ghosting until I started dating. Now I am quite famil-iar. When we don't know what to say or have the skills we need to say it, we simply disappear.

I really dislike this about us.

Perhaps you have a visceral reaction when a friend mentions being ghosted. Or maybe your feelings are stronger when you think of folks you have ghosted. Or maybe, like many of us, you feel equally gross when considering either one.

So why do we do it?

My answer? That's the wrong question. The

better question is: how do we stop? And what do we do when we are ghosted? If you want to get into your whys, chat with your therapist. If you want to get into someone else's motivation, you are in for a long winter. They ghosted you. This means they're unlikely to want to sit down and have the meta-conversation about why *with you*.

The Space Between

The expanse between ghosts and monsters contains a few options that may better align with your boundaries:

- Monster
- Acknowledgement
- Arrangement
- Closing
- Ghosting

The **monster** says too much, too fast, with no consideration. The **ghost** says nothing—sometimes because of too much consideration, other times because consideration feels painful. There are options in between, depending on which demon you're trying to avoid.

Acknowledgement is the first step when the monster takes hold.

"I got your message," is an acknowledgement. Sometimes an added statement like "I'm unable to respond now" is quite appropriate. These are good scripts. Put them in a note on your phone right now.

Other times, a detail like "I need time to process" is a useful addition. Then hand the phone off or put it in the freezer. Step away from anywhere you could react and consult support before responding.

Arrangement is often a great next step when the text monster is lurking. Text is a terrible way to communicate emotion and nuance. It is great for logistics but otherwise it's a strong argument for spoken rather than written language. Instead of getting into an emotive and detailed debate via text, consider arranging a different form of communication. "I got your message. Can we find a time to chat on the phone? I think voice communication will be better for me than texting about this." You can also establish a timeline for further communication. After acknowledging receipt, you can arrange that you will respond via a particular method at a certain time. "I need to sleep on this, so you can expect a reply from me tomorrow evening."

Sometimes **closing** is the appropriate response. If your ghosting behavior stems from wanting to end a relationship, might I suggest closing instead? Think of putting a bow on it, or graduating, if either of those concepts is helpful—simple, direct, mature, and responsive (rather than reactive). I got quite clear in my dating experiences and created a method and script for my responses because I did not want to waste emotional energy considering each case unique. That would have resulted in ghosting on my part.

While your defense against the text monster might be to delete and block a contact, cutting off all further communication (ghosting), that's rarely appropriate.

And here's where I get to say you'll need to consult a real, live, breathing human (or three) in each circumstance.

If someone I hadn't met in person and had only interacted with online said something offensive or off-putting, I would ghost. In my case, if they sent me an unsolicited picture of their genitals, it was an automatic delete/block, the same way I would run across the street if someone flashed me in public. This is purple list behavior—it's illegal in public, and if your objective is actual dating and not just sex, it's not the way to introduce yourself.

If they said something that was on my deal-breakers (red) list, I would respond with a one-liner indicating such and end the conversation. "Thanks for the chat. I don't date Geminis, so I'm ending the conversation."

Once a relationship is established, closing can be a little bit more difficult because they often want to know why. If you've gone on five dates with someone and then decide you're not a match, they are likely to ask you about it. And this is where real maturity comes in. First, you do not have to tell them. You can decide to end any relationship at any point without justification (unless you are legally required to provide care for the other person, as in your juvenile children). It's rather awkward to ghost a marriage after a few years, but I do firmly believe that you do not *owe* anyone an explanation. I do believe that the ending is an opportunity not to justify but to clarify who you are in the moment you are departing the relationship.

Second, if you'd like to practice skillful closing, I suggest chatting with a mentor or two first and then crafting the most compassionate statement you can, defining the relationship and articulating how it has migrated out of the green zone. Agree on a first line to start the conversation and write a script. For me, a script is the most important place to start.

"It's been lovely getting to know you, but I'm interested in finding someone who loves Renaissance festivals as much as I do," is great after three dates. You can even tell them what you learned about them in the process that might be helpful on their next step, "I wish I loved sword swallowing as much as you do, but I'm confident there are some enthusiastic folks out there."

After a longer relationship, this gets hard. So hard, I'm not sure I'm fully capable of stating it for the record. But the process is the same. Identify what is red/yellow/green (and purple). Talk with some trusted people and create a script to start with the conversation. Frame it as a graduation, as though one chapter is complete and another is beginning.

And listen. You might learn something about yourself.

If you intend for this to be the last conversation you have with this person, make it count. Do not be vindictive. Consider if they were to die soon afterwards, whether you could be at peace with what you said. Speak from that place.

"I have to tell you something that will be hard for you to hear," is a great first line, whether you're in the casual dating place or have crossed into long-term commitment. It is true and valid, and it isn't a negotiation. You are ready for the relationship to end, or be redefined, and that is true no matter what or how the other person feels.

Then, if you are ready, you listen.

Our lessons follow us around until we're ready to learn them. We will repeat the same behaviors, mistakes and patterns until we're ready to try something different. I think this is good news. If you're at the place where you're considering ending a relationship, it's because you've recognized something about yourself. Maybe that you want to be treated differently. Maybe you have different aspirations, or more clarity. You've discerned some red and some green based on the time invested, and that's worth holding onto as you decide to move forwards. If you ghost, you cheat yourself out of the mirror of the other side of this lesson.

Let me say that again.

If you ghost, you are cheating yourself.

The other person's experience of you is valid. It may not resonate with you, you may not understand it, and frankly, there are times when it has nothing to do with you. But more often, there is something there. If you make a habit of ghosting, you are not giving yourself the opportunity to hear a pattern develop.

You might find yourself lost in the same loop, unaware and drowning in your own ignorance.

For example, if all of your exes complain about your apparent need for personal space, maybe you need to look at that. Do you actually require more personal space than you are communicating up front? Or maybe you are choosing to partner with people who need a lot of attention and reassurance and prefer their partner to meet all those needs. Adorable pattern, and so common there are entire books written about it.

Maybe your friends always sign off because they feel you have asked for things without reciprocating— you always seemed to call in crisis and were not around to listen when they were experiencing something stressful. This has happened to me, and it showed me how bad my life had become. I had not realized I was constantly complaining or in crisis until I found myself without friends who would answer the phone.

Was I always choosing to be friends with jerks?

Not precisely, but I was choosing a few toxic people who made my reasonable friends skitter out pronto. The others were operating in toxic land, and I was wooed by their crises. So much to manage, so little time to focus on my own work and worth. What a relief.

Once you hear the lesson you're repeating, you get to do something different about it. At the end of this relationship, you have the opportunity to say:

"I need so much personal space, and you need so much togetherness,"

or:

"I have this handy group of fellows who I consult in a crisis, and it seems you don't have your own group of fellows and are hoping/expecting that one solitary person (me) will help you manage it all."

And then wish them well, put a bow on the conversation and be clear about how you wish to handle future communications.

"I'd love to reconnect next February,"

or:

"I'd like to stick to logistics via this email account,"

or:

"I'm not interested in future correspondence."

I decided many years ago that my lowest acceptable standard for ending a relationship was to do it in a way that leaves room for us to be cordial in five years. I don't want to engage in relationships where I am triggered by seeing a familiar name or running into someone on the subway in a city where neither of us live (this sort of thing happens in my life). That lets the other person have power over me. If, instead, I end the conversation with clarity and good wishes, I'm more likely to see someone and feel nostalgic or neutral.

This is true even if I am not open to future correspondence, with very few exceptions.

It is possible there are people in your life with whom you should not engage at all—ever. Some folks are so sick they cannot respect boundaries and will launch themselves at you in any way they can. I have experienced this, so it is on good authority I suggest engaging the expertise of your HC and possibly adding a whole category to guide you in creating a strong boundary with someone you must place on the purple list. In my life, I have experienced significant compassion for people who have done me irreparable harm. This compassion has been a problem for me. I'm a champion at seeing the hurt child inside of a person who is hurting me. Then I give them many, many more opportunities to change (and hurt me) than they deserve. I stay too long in relationships that hurt me.

That is my lesson.

I have created an army in my higher council to keep me honest and help me separate my trauma from my reality, my intuition from flashbacks. I say this so those who share this experience know they are not alone. It is also important for those partnering, friending or working with someone who has a history of trauma to appreciate the delicate nature of their experience.

The moral of the end of relationships is that all the wrong people in your life are there to show you who the right people are.

Why We Ghost

Okay fine. Now that you're through that bit, let's look at the reasons we ghost. But first, you must promise not to get lost in the rabbit hole of why someone ghosted you. You won't know. You can't know. They ghosted. That's the thing. You can make up an answer if that helps you sleep better at night. You can only be responsible for identifying your own ghosting behavior. This is really wonderful to do, because if you can identify it, you can be more selective about when and how you ghost, knowing you are only cheating yourself if you do.

Yes, even on the purple list. (And maybe especially there, but we will get to it.)

We Ghost When We Are Speechless

Surprise, dismay, or offense might be the first reactions we have when we hear a nasty rumor about ourselves. Someone believes and is sharing a significant untruth, and we are blindsided and have no idea how to respond. I remember feeling this when a manager at work started a rumor that I was stealing, and when a partner strung together some disconnected thoughts and assumed I was seeing someone else. I was shocked and unsure of how to proceed. Surely, we've been warned about protesting too much, but we have no template for how to respond when we feel we have no appropriate response.

How do I tell my employer I've been completely transparent with my money handling and, in many cases, have spent my own money on supplies?

How do I tell my partner I haven't been seeing or even conversing with anyone else when their past experiences with cheating seem to be informing this moment?

How do I prove my innocence? I know my words will be used against me, so I swallow them, which, in certain cases, equates to ghosting.

Adorable, right?

What if we had a tiny script to close the relationship or define the green instead?

"It has come to my attention you are sharing false statements about me. I feel betrayed, and I ask my friends to come to me directly with concerns. I'm not interested in further communication with you."

Maybe you'll add something about corresponding via your lawyer if a situation, such as my work issue, warrants it.

And maybe you could ask for an opportunity to speak in person or on the phone about these rumors if you're not ready to end that relationship.

We Ghost to Avoid Confronting the Truth

My therapist once said to me that we partner with people who are as available as we are. I misremembered it and re-wrote it in my journal as "we partner with people who are equally fucked up as we are," and I agree with my misquote as well as her original statement. Hers was relative to the fact that I liked to date people who were at least 60 nautical miles away from me, though preferably closer to 1,000.

Mine, I fear, is also true.

If you get to the point in a friendship or relationship where you believe you are in cahoots with one another, the other person is often a brilliant mirror. They represent the match to your puzzle piece in some way. It's then up to you to know if it's an authentic match—as in are they matching the real you or the you that you're projecting. The truth is always liberating, whether the truth is that we're fabricating a self or running away from one. But that doesn't mean we're open to truth. We're often not ready or willing to accept it because most of us are not Spock, and we do not operate from logic even if we wish we could.

Maybe the truth is you simply cannot make peace with their cat, which they feel is an extension of themselves. You cannot continue to listen to your friend's stories of sowing wild oats and leaving a trail of wreckage. Maybe the truth is your sexuality is inconsistent with theirs. Or with them.

We Ghost Because We Fear the Recipient's Reaction

You probably don't want to make people feel bad, so you mistakenly believe your lack of action will be better than your action. Like Thumper in *Bambi,* you believe it is better to say nothing if you have nothing nice to say. But when we reflect on our experience of being ghosted, we are rarely grateful that the person simply vanished without closing the relationship.

We can consider the script we use and whether it passes through Buddhism's three gates: is it true, kind, and necessary? These are gorgeous gates. Rather than saying nothing, consider crafting a script based on these guiding principles. Speak the truth kindly and say only the parts that are necessary. This takes effort and courage, which is emotionally expensive. It is work, but it is work that is worth it, because doing the work now means you will not have to do it in future relationships. You will have the experience—the precedent—of speaking your truth and surviving it.

If the person is likely to erupt and become angry, sad, or otherwise emotional, consider what feels safest to you. If the person is abusive, hurting you or someone else, this chapter does not apply (because the book doesn't apply, remember?). But if the person is likely to be emotional in a way you won't be able to manage, you have options. Saying something doesn't mean face-to-face in a coffee shop or town square with credits rolling and dramatic music. Saying something can be done many ways, including a postcard with no return address, an email, or some other low-contact method. You will share some aspect of your truth and will have walked the three gates. You will benefit, learning through your own courage and effort. And you won't have to receive feedback from the person, unless you invite or make space for a response.

We Ghost Unintentionally

Once in my fledgling dating career, I dated a man who lost his phone. We had been seeing each other for five months and set aside the weekend to spend together. I heard nothing from him. He went to a work function Friday and had to wait for the business to open on Monday to retrieve the device. He simply did not communicate this to me via any means.

I was understanding and forgiving at the time—which was ridiculous. He had been to my house before, and if you haven't noticed, my name is really quite unique. It's super Googleable—and I have a website that is my name, as well as Twitter, Facebook and Instagram accounts and a multitude of other ways to communicate. These days, if you know a few details about someone, it's pretty easy to send a message. Sometimes, technology is brilliant and provides us ways to connect and close relationships with ease. Other times, it gets in the way.

I have a friend who attempted to send a closure message via a dating app and then disconnected, erasing both the message and the capacity to locate the person in the future. Oops. This happens, and it's helpful for us to remember this when we are ghosted. Sometimes the mail does not get through or the message is lost in cyberspace.

That's a potential downside of closing without face-to-face or voice communication. Sometimes we change phone numbers or lose track. Sometimes people are assholes. Sometimes I'm the asshole. *So, know your tendencies and be selective about how you invest your compassion, my darling.*

We Die

The source of the term "ghosted" is, I'm sure, the unlikely possibility that the person who ghosted you actually died.

This happened to me.

So, I know it happens and I know what it feels like. I know how it feels to get really mad at someone, then hurt. Then you move on, only to have them visit you in a dream seven years later, which inspires you to Google them, and you learn they are in fact deceased.

I know how it is to experience guilt for feeling mad that they wouldn't return a phone call, cursing their existence, wishing them ill and then learning your curse was too late.

I also know how it feels to leave a relationship without proper closure and in the arms of another. I regret it still. Hence, I write books. I assure you, closing the relationship via text, postcard, or carrier pigeon would have been preferable to knowing that the last memory he had of me was worse than ghosting.

Dear Jon,

I'm sorry I walked away from you in tears, in the arms of another man, and didn't have the skills or integrity to speak my full truth.

I aim to live differently.

Interlude: Synchronicity

I never wanted to go to India.

The first time I saluted the sun was ankle-deep in crab grass outside of my Kindergarten classroom, in a time before mats and yoga pants, and it was in part because my bearded hippie teacher had spent some time wandering in that spiritual well.

Even so, and after a degree in anthropology, she never called to me.

India is chaotic and messy and provides none of the artificial guarantees that have lined the borders of my sanity in the West. She operates by her own rules.

So, when my boss invited me to accompany him on a trip and have the experience of her, I politely declined.

When my friend and co-worker (and photographer) who was going suggested I join him and perhaps we venture to India a few days early for sightseeing in Delhi, I politely declined.

When my ex-husband mentioned that he was in Northern India at a language school, and that his employer, a Buddhist

Rinpoche, might be taking audience with His Holiness the Dalai Lama in that same timeframe, I paused, and declined.

When I ran into my former boss, who happens to be the former US Ambassador to India, at a restaurant late one night, years after our working relationship had ended, and he told me that he still follows my writing and if I ever wanted to go to India he could make all of the right connections, I stopped.

The Universe is sometimes so subtle in the ways that paths cross or signs line up to create significance, but this was not one of those times.

I had a friend who wanted to pay for my trip. Another friend wanted to accompany me. Another could introduce me to HH The Dalai Lama, and another would connect me with a cultural attaché who had previously hosted people with the last name of Kennedy, should I be interested.

None of this felt subtle.

In fact, it represented in odd and perfect detail, my infinites-imally small green list of India (to the letter). More than a signpost on the road or a subtle cairn, it was a neon sign that fell on my head.

And I went.

I learned many things in India—to walk confidently at my own pace, to clear the path of my adorable plans and instead live according to my values, to consider time as something simul-taneous rather than linear. To revere the land whose story is told by the qualities of water. To watch for synchronicities and make green lists.

Conclusion

You are already perfect.

That's not a message you're likely to hear every day unless you say it to yourself. Your feelings, emotions, ideas, and preferences are perfect. You can address your behaviors with the tools in your toolkit. You are responsible for them and to them, and that is the great news. You can be proud of your actions and sleep well knowing you spoke or acted in integrity with the support of tools and counselors.

Your relationships will never be perfect—mine aren't. The work isn't something you finish. My wish for you is that you decide never to settle for life on the orange line—that you see life as a potential place to explore green, an infinite well of counselors on any subject, limited only by your ability to see your life as an exploration of yourself and your boundaries. Consider that your boundaries do not confine you, but are your invitation to expand to the farthest reaches and map the full territory of yourself.

If you need it, take the lifeboat of recovery. Get simple and tidy and then seek out shores that render the lifeboat unnecessary.

Keep the recovery.

Your relationships and tendencies will show you how the world connects to you will and allow you to be honest and authentic. This will likely mean ending relationships. While this takes courage, it does not require the bracing and fear you might expect. Every time the wrong person crosses your path, they give you information about who the right person is. You can thank them for highlighting a dimension of you and then start over in hot pursuit of the right job, friendship, or partnership.

After reading this book, you have recipes for joy and intimacy and antidotes for resentment and drama. You might be surprised to discover that life with less chaos can be more interesting and fulfilling. More opportunities for magic and synchronicity will reveal themselves as you know and articulate what you want often and loudly, and new circumstances present evolving opportunities to refine.

Live your life guided by joy and the green list. Let it expand to the fullness of you.

Live a life worth writing about.

Then write about it.

Epilogue

Boundaries in the time of pandemics and a global awakening around racism.

I'm writing this bit under a waning moon, at 5:30 in the morning on July 8, 2020. While nothing else in this book is time-stamped, this moment feels important because life is evolving in ways I have never experienced, and I want you to know the date in case another seismic moment transpires between my now and yours.

I believe all things have equal capacity for good and evil—the most amazing can be the most terrible, and I believe that to be true of this pandemic. It has the capacity for tremendous destruction, which includes within it the opportunity for something big to be created. During the shelter at home, our boundaries were defined for us, and once this was lifted, I received dozens of memos from Better Boundaries alumni detailing the ways these tools had been helpful in navigating new decisions about where to go and how to engage during a global pandemic.

Based on this, I believe the tools to be quite helpful and I want to add the following note: *if something feels impossible to categorize or compromise about, it likely needs to be broken down into smaller pieces.*

For example, should we cancel our family trip to Florida? Feels like a simple question, but the answer is hard. At this writing, Florida is the biggest hot spot for the virus, and restrictions are coming and going by the minute. Consider the motivations to go. Consider a question that is bigger and more focused on what feels green: is this the best time to go to Florida? What would feel most green about it?

The answers depend on circumstances, like how you feel and whether you have had an antibody test. If you'll go for a month and can quarantine in the guest house for 14 days after you arrive. If you drive versus fly. Might I suggest creating a section of your HC for pandemic travel? Make a bingo card? How many of these tools can you throw at this novel problem?

In recent weeks, so much has also shifted in our shared awareness of racism and anti-racism, and this is the other area where alumni of Boundaries are finding these tools helpful. If you are the person who has suffered the experience of racism, you may benefit from an area of your HC that specifically supports that. There are authors, teachers, and coaches whose voices may resonate with you. You are not in any way required to mentor anyone about racism unless it is a calling for you and you feel well-supported in this area of your life. It may be helpful to create a green/red list about talking about racism, what you're willing to do, and what you're unwilling to do. Your experience is valid, and the added burden of unpacking white privilege is not your responsibility.

If you have benefitted from white privilege, you might consider devoting a section of your HC to anti-racism. You'll need peers, mentors, and professionals in the field, not simply the presence of racial diversity on your HC. Locating a black friend and asking them to take on the responsibility of educating you about your privilege is not HC work. Finding professionals is relatively easy—they often publish books and offer courses you can take. From there, you can start to locate peers and mentors. I implore you to build out your HC in this area right now. It will help you prioritize and identify those who support deactivating our cultural willingness to allow racism to perpetuate. The work you do in this area will have a legacy, conscious or otherwise.

Leave a great legacy.

Acknowledgments

Truly the most terrifying aspect of writing this book is this section. I am bound to forget some people whose influence has been vital to the project, or my mental health, or the publication process.

My teachers are both those who have sat at the front of the room, and those who have kicked me when I was down. While I am most certainly not grateful in each of those cases, I acknowledge that they have been part of the story that landed me here, in this moment.

This book is dedicated to Hannah, my Dharma, which feels quite poetic to me as I consider the yogic meaning of the term and how perspective is my purpose. I am honoring both the person who answered the phone and read the love letters I never sent to their intended recipients, and the greater purpose of my life.

For Katie Wise, whose presence introduced me to Courtney Love and Alexis Koutoulakos, whose votes of support and cosmic wonder introduced me to Yoshi Aono, who granted me the role to meet Tommy Rosen & Kia Miller, who introduced me to my own addictive tendencies as well as DJ Pierce, Sukhdev and Akahdahmah Jackson and Nikki Myers. In the darkest and shadowed moments, this crew of souls reminded me that the recipe for a shadow includes a light source, and that perhaps I might turn around, shift my perspective, and paddle towards the light.

For Ryan Sharp, whose wisdom is quiet and resolve a force for gravity, whose vision centered me and kept me tethered to the earth, and Carly Beaudin whose insight asked me many hard questions and connected me to many right steps. For Patrick & Cameron Harrington, Karen Munna, the Sha-wo-man, and Govinda, who maybe did not know that I was hanging by a thread in the moments they invited me out of my primordial healing nest in Costa Rica, but did.

For Anna David, my publisher, who was weirdly enthusiastic about me even though I'm just me, and Becky Sasso, the editor of editors who can make sense out of the mess of my psychic overspray and sort it into A Book.

For Sophie & Adam and your littles, Bea, Jen W., Jen G., Suzanne, Splendor, Michelle, Tara, Cyndi, Kevin, Heidika, The Angelator, Kimberly, Lindsay G., Jessica C. Patterson and the myriad others who provided meals, shoulders, airport pickups and stops along the way. For Maggie who taught me how to fish, and how to speak up for myself, and never shied away from saying so when someone needed to say so.

And of course, for Bob, Natalia, Kathleen, Andrew, and Ben who stood by me equally as I was married and divorced, and helped me to understand how to heal rather than simply paint over again.

For my countless and nameless siblings and sponsors in recovery who answered the phone or nodded with understanding.

For Lilah, who represents hope.

For my parents and my ancestors, who understand and echo through me, whose footprints are next to mine on every step of my wild journey.

And for Aaron, who reminds me that I am stronger than I think I am.

And loves me anyway.

CPSIA information can be obtained
at www.ICGtesting.com
Printed in the USA
FSHW011433271120
76307FS